Fresh Blends

a nourishing blend of recipes

Nutrition related tips and suggestions are provided for your information and are not intended as medical advice. For specific questions regarding your individual health or diet, please consult your medical professional to determine what is right for you.

Every recipe in this book has been prepared in our test kitchen using the Total Blender®. The Blendtec test kitchen is located in Orem, Utah and is approximately 4,800 feet above sea level. This elevation is important to note since changes in elevation may affect the outcome of the recipes (specifically baked goods). Please keep in mind that as elevation increases, air pressure decreases. Decreased air pressure affects food preparation in two ways: leavening gases in bread and cakes expand more quickly, and, water and other liquids boil and evaporate faster at lower temperatures.

Contact:
1-800-748-5400

Mon — Fri, 8:00 am — 5:30 pm
Mountain Standard Time
Blendtec Corporate Offices
1206 West 1680 South
Orem, Utah 84058

To register the warranty on your machine, view recipes, and to watch informational videos, please visit us online at www.blendtec.com.

Congratulations on the purchase of your Blendtec® Blender! Get ready to enjoy everything from beverages to breads, soups to sauces and frozen treats to raw food recipes.

The Blending Basics section will take you through various applications to demonstrate the complete spectrum of the Blender's functionality including various tips and techniques to be used during recipe preparation. Please take time to review the Blending Basics section to help you get started and discover all the culinary possibilities now available to you! Please visit us online at www.blendtec.com for additional recipes and instructional videos.

We are here for you! At Blendtec, we constantly place customer satisfaction as one of our top priorities; we are committed to making your blending experience the best possible. If you have any questions regarding your new Blender, we are here to answer them. Do not hesitate to call customer service at 1-800-748-5400 or contact us online through Facebook, Twitter or on our site.

While this book contains some great recipes and ideas, it is by no means all inclusive. We ask that as you use your Blendtec Blender you share with us suggestions, tips, recipes or other ideas by sending an email to recipes@blendtec.com. We wish you every success, ease and enjoyment as you now discover your new Blendtec Blender.

Long before the Will It Blend™ series exploded on YouTube, Tom Dickson was blending 2 x 2s with his blenders to determine their capabilities. As an engineer and inventor, Tom grew up putting big engines in little things.

Back in 1975, Tom's curiosity came between a vacuum and some spilled wheat berries. His innate inquisitiveness drove him to revolutionize the home wheat milling industry taking it from stone grinding to his patented stainless steel milling heads. Like most inventors, Tom did not stop here; he envisioned the perfect mixer using the freshly milled flour from his mill to make wholesome bread in minutes. While back in the lab, Tom developed the auto-knead button allowing the mixer to knead the dough, develop the gluten, and turn off automatically when finished. Tom continued to improve the mixer and decided to add a blender with a square jar, rather than the conventional round shaped jar. As Tom grew his mill and mixer business, new ideas developed and he enhanced the blender and began developing commercial blending machines just as the smoothie era began.

Fast forward to today, Tom is still inventing and the company is still growing! Walking into the world of Team Blendtec, you will find the innovative engineering team and their "Torture Chamber," the international team seeing where their travels take them next and you will still find Tom around the plant scooting off to blend up his next invention.

Today, people all around the world use Blendtec blenders in their homes, restaurants, smoothie shops, coffee shops and more. We continue to develop new and better ways to build machines that improve the lives of others. It all began with one man and his curiosity. He has shared that vision with others and the dream continues to unfold.

Table of Contents

Blending Basics

Blending Basics

Blender Components

FourSide Jar: Blendtec's BPA-free, patented, 4-sided jar measures up to 32 fl oz with a volume of 74 fl oz. This jar is great for smaller yielding recipes as well as sauces, dressings and nut butters.

WildSide Jar: Blendtec's BPA-free, patented, 5-sided jar measures up to 36 fl oz with a volume of 90 fl oz. This jar has a larger base which increases surface area. The fifth side offsets the blending vortex resulting in improved blending performance and reduced possibility of cavitation (where an air pocket forms above the blade). This jar is great for larger yielding recipes as well as yeast breads, quick breads and frozen desserts.

Vented Gripper Lid and Insert: Allows steam to escape while blending warm contents or during a long cycle. Removing the lid insert makes it easy to add ingredients while blending.

Spline Shaft

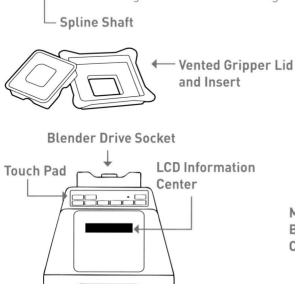

Vented Gripper Lid and Insert

Blender Drive Socket

Touch Pad

LCD Information Center

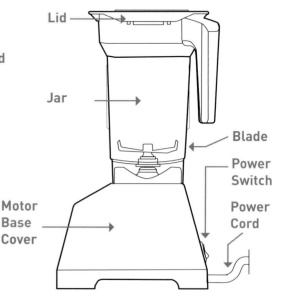

Lid

Jar

Blade

Power Switch

Power Cord

Motor Base Cover

LCD Information Center: The LCD screen displays the specific cycle selected and then displays the countdown, in seconds, before your recipe is ready to enjoy!

Blade: Stainless steel, two-prong, wingtip design ensures a smooth consistent blend.

Blender Drive Socket: The spline shaft fits in the drive socket which is part of the motor; the steel on steel, direct-drive design allows for the most torque which results in better blending results.

Blender Motor Base and Touch Pad Controls: This recipe book is designed for use with both the Total Blender® and Home Blender® from Blendtec. Both blenders use the same motor and have pre-programmed blend cycles. These pre-programmed settings save time, are easy to use, and promise consistent results every time. Below are the differences between the Total Blender and Home Blender touchpads.

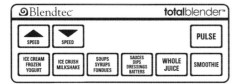

The Total Blender has six pre-programmed blend cycles as well as the manual controls of "Speed Up", "Speed Down"and "Pulse." All Total Blender users please note, when following a recipe and it states to "Select" a specific cycle, you will press the correlating button on the touch pad.

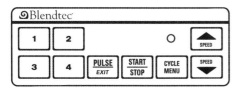

The Home Blender has 25 pre-programmed blend cycles as well as the manual controls for "Speed Up", "Speed Down" and "Pulse". All Home Blender users please note, when following a recipe and it states to "Select" a specific cycle, press the cycle menu button and press "Speed Up"or "Speed Down" to find the specific cycle in the menu; then press "Start". The buttons numbered 1, 2, 3 and 4 are for you to select from the 25 pre-programmed cycles or to program the button with the cycle of your choice. To select the cycle of your choice, search in the cycle menu, find the desired cycle, press the numbered button of choice and hold it down until the machine beeps indicating that programming is complete.

Cleaning and Care

Jar:

Before using your blender jar for the first time, add 1-2 cups warm water to your jar. Add a drop of liquid dishwashing soap and secure lid. Place the jar on the motor base and press "Pulse" and hold for 5–10 seconds. Remove jar; rinse both jar and lid thoroughly.

To ensure maximum jar life, please follow the instructions below:

- Do not store food in the jar or soak the jar in any liquid for an extended period of time.
- After each use, wash the jar and lid. Please note, some thick mixtures, such as bread dough and nut butters, may require additional hand washing.
- When the jar is not used daily, the internal seal may become stuck to the jar. If so, we recommend that before use, you add a ½ cup warm water to the jar. Then reach under the bottom of the jar and twist the spline shaft for a few seconds. Empty the jar and then fill with recipe ingredients.
- During blending, some vibration is normal; there is no need to hold or jiggle the jar.
- The 7 year warranty on the jar(s) does not cover cosmetic alterations. Blending coffee, spices, herbs, etc., may discolor the jar and the scent may penetrate the material of the jar. We recommend purchasing specific jars for these purposes. As a side note, blending hard grains, such as wheat and rice, may cause interior pitting of the jar surface resulting in a "fogged" appearance; this is not covered under warranty.

Motor Base:

- Always turn the rocker switch (located on the back side of the motor base) to the off position and unplug the power cord before cleaning.
- Wipe down the motor base cover with a damp cloth or sponge which has been rinsed in a mild solution of dish soap and warm water.
- Dry the motor base cover with a soft cloth.
- Please refer to the Care and Cleaning Section in your owner's manual for more specific cleaning instructions and tips.

Applications
Simple Recipes to Get You Started

⊙ Blending: The simple act of blending can be used to make smoothies, blend batters, smooth soups, emulsify salad dressings and mix drinks.

Mixed Fruit Smoothie

A refreshing fruit smoothie bursting with flavor and packed with Vitamin C.

FourSide Jar
1 C grapes
1 orange
1 banana
1 C strawberries
2 C ice cubes

Add ingredients to jar in order listed and secure lid. Select "Smoothie" and serve.

Whipped Cream

Quick and easy whipped cream ready in seconds to adorn any dessert.

FourSide Jar
1 C whipping cream
1 Tbsp powdered sugar
½ tsp vanilla extract

Add ingredients to jar in order listed and secure lid. Press "Speed Up" to Speed 1, run cycle for 15–20 seconds and press "Pulse" to stop cycle. Using a spatula, move contents towards center of jar and secure lid. Press "Pulse" for 1–2 seconds. Move contents towards center of jar with spatula. Continue pulsing and stirring 1–2 more times until desired consistency is reached. Yields: 2 cups.

For Chocolate Whipped Cream, follow instructions above and add 1 tablespoon cocoa powder and an additional 2 tablespoons of powdered sugar to the whipping cream and vanilla extract.

Banana Bread

Whipping up this traditional banana bread recipe in the blender cuts prep time significantly.

*WildSide Jar
2 ripe bananas, approximately 1 C mashed
2 lg eggs
½ C low-fat vanilla yogurt
¾ C granulated or turbinado sugar
¼ C coconut oil
½ tsp vanilla extract
1 ½ C all-purpose or whole wheat flour
1 tsp baking soda
1 tsp kosher salt

Preheat oven to 350°F. Add first 6 ingredients to jar and secure lid. Select "Batters". Add remaining ingredients and secure lid. Press "Pulse" 3–5 times until dry ingredients are incorporated; do not over blend. Pour batter into greased 9"x 5" loaf pan. Bake for 50–60 minutes.

*To prepare this recipe in the FourSide jar, first add flour, baking soda and salt to jar and secure lid. Press "Pulse" 3–5 times to sift dry ingredients. Add sifted dry ingredients to a mixing bowl. Add remaining ingredients to jar and secure lid. Select "Batters". Pour wet ingredients into bowl with dry ingredients; mix to combine. Pour batter into 9"x 5" loaf pan. Bake for 50–60 minutes.

☺ Wet Chopping: Wet chopping is a convenient and easy way of chopping by using water to circulate the ingredients in the jar. After straining, keep the liquid for use in smoothies, sauces and soups.

Chopping Cabbage

Either Jar
4 chunks cabbage, approximately 2 C

Add cabbage to jar, fill with enough water to cover the cabbage and secure lid. Press "Pulse" 8–12 times until desired texture is reached. Pour contents of jar over mesh strainer; allow to drain.

Note: You can add carrots or cilantro to jar at the same time for a crunchy coleslaw salad.

☺ Wet Grinding: Grinding foods that contain moisture such as nuts, soaked grains and meat is best ground in small to medium batches.

Grinding Meat

It is so easy to grind raw meat for meatballs or shred cooked meat for chicken salad.

	FourSide	WildSide
raw meat, cubed	½ lb	1 lb
cooked meat, cubed	½ lb	1 lb

Add cubed meat to jar and secure lid. Press "Pulse" 4–6 times until ground to desired consistency.

☻ Juicing Whole Foods: Whole food juice delivers all the health benefits of both the juice and the fiber found in the fruit and/or vegetable. The Blendtec Blender breaks the whole food fiber into microscopic pieces that are easy to digest making nutrients easier to absorb.

Total Juice

A common whole juice blend used by Blendtec representatives at live demonstrations.

Either Jar
2 C grapes, seeded or seedless
¼ orange
3 strawberries
1 slice pineapple, rind removed
1 slice cantaloupe, rind removed
½ kiwi
¼ apple, cored
½ C ice cubes

Add ingredients to jar in order listed and secure lid. Select "Whole Juice" and serve.

Try adding a few leafy greens, such as spinach or kale, to increase the nutrient density of this juice without increasing the number of carbohydrates.

☻ Dry Chopping: The Blendtec Blender is convenient for chopping nuts, hard cheeses, coconut, etc. By using your blender to complete these tasks, they become easy, quick and require less clean-up. Chop ingredients in small batches for best results. Use the manual controls "Pulse", "Speed Up" and "Speed Down" to chop. Please note the texture and piece size change as blending time is increased or as you change from a higher to lower speed.

Chopping Nuts

To chop nuts separate from other ingredients, place nuts in the FourSide jar and secure lid. Press "Speed Up" to Speed 2 and run for 5–25 seconds depending on the temperature, tenderness and amount of nuts.

Note: The majority of blender chopped nuts have a semi-uniform size while a small portion are chopped very finely and pushed into the corners of the jar or under the blade. The amount of nuts for optimal chopping in the FourSide jar is ¾ –1 cup.

Parmesan Cheese

FourSide Jar
½ lb wedge cold Parmesan cheese, cubed to 1" pieces

Secure lid and remove vented gripper lid insert press "Speed Up" to Speed 4, drop Parmesan cheese cubes into blender and quickly replace insert. Process cheese for 15–20 seconds and press "Pulse" to stop cycle; do not over blend.

....

❂ Dry Grinding: The Blendtec Blender can crack or grind legumes and whole grains for use in hot cereals, baked goods, and breads. Grinding your own grains offers fresh taste and nutritional benefits found in the whole grain.

....

Powdered Sugar

Whether you need a little to dust over dessert or enough to make frosting, this is a quick and easy way to create your own powdered sugar in seconds.

FourSide Jar
1 C granulated sugar*

Place jar on blender base, secure lid and remove the vented gripper lid insert. Select "Batters", quickly add sugar and replace the vented gripper lid insert to prevent powdered sugar blowing through the vent. Once cycle is complete, use as desired; store powdered sugar in an airtight container.

Note: Several commercial varieties may contain cornstarch to prevent caking. To duplicate this effect, add 1 tablespoon cornstarch with the sugar when blending.

*For a less refined powdered sugar option, substitute granulated sugar for sucanat or turbinado sugar and follow the above instructions.

Ice Crush

Use shaved ice for a summer time snow cone soirée or to chill drinks. For snow cones, add fresh fruit syrup or thawed fruit juice concentrate in condiment squeeze bottles to enjoy the refreshment without the artificial flavor.

FourSide Jar*
3 C ice cubes

Add ice cubes to jar and secure lid. Select "Ice Crush". For best results, use ice cubes directly from freezer that have not begun to melt.

*If using the WildSide jar, increase ice cubes to 5 cups.

Cracking Whole Grains

FourSide Jar
2 C wheat berries

Add wheat berries to jar and secure lid. Press "Speed Up" to Speed 4, run for 8–10 seconds and press "Pulse" to stop cycle. If a finer consistency is desired, continue to blend for a few more seconds. Remember longer processing will result in flour.

See the "Grinding Grains" section (pg 124–125) for more information on cracking wheat and other grains.

Whole Wheat Flour

FourSide Jar
2 C wheat berries

Add wheat berries to jar and secure lid. Press "Speed Up" to Speed 9 and run full cycle. Yields: 2 ⅔ cups flour.

See the "Grinding Grains" section (pg 124–125) for more details in grinding wheat and other grains.

Homemade Bread Crumbs

The Blendtec Blender is perfect for crushing graham crackers into cookie crumbs or chopping bread into bread crumbs effortlessly. Whole grain bread crumbs are great to have on hand whether you want to make meatballs or need a few bread crumbs to thicken soup.

Either Jar
4 slices bread

Toast 4 bread slices in a toaster or oven. Quarter bread slices, place in jar and secure lid. Press "Speed Up" to Speed 1, run for 10–15 seconds and press "Pulse" to stop cycle.

For Italian Bread Crumbs, add the following herbs to the jar before blending the toasted bread:
½ **tsp dried parsley flakes**
½ **tsp garlic powder**
½ **tsp kosher salt**
¼ **tsp dried oregano**
¼ **tsp dried basil**
¼ **tsp onion powder**
¼ **tsp ground black pepper**

◉ Kneading: After grinding your whole grains into flour use the same jar to transform your flour and wet ingredients into fresh whole grain dough in one smooth operation. The blade incorporates the wet and dry ingredients and kneads the dough until a dough ball forms that is ready to rise and bake.

Whole Wheat Naan

A simple and straightforward way to make a leavened Indian flat bread using nearly 100% whole wheat flour. This bread is delicious served with your favorite curry dish or sliced and served with hummus.

WildSide Jar
⅓ C milk, warmed
2 ¼ tsp dry active yeast
½ Tbsp sugar
¾ C plain yogurt
2 Tbsp canola oil
1 ½ tsp kosher salt
¼ tsp baking powder
2 C whole white wheat flour
½ C all-purpose flour

Add first 3 ingredients to jar and secure lid. Press "Pulse" 2 times and allow the yeast to proof for 5–10 minutes. Combine flours in a separate bowl. Add next 4 ingredients and ⅓ of flour and secure lid. Press "Pulse" 2–3 times. Add next ⅓ of flour and secure lid. Press "Pulse" 3-5 times. Add the last ⅓ of flour and secure lid. Press "Pulse" 6–8 times until all flour is incorporated and dough ball forms. Let dough rest and rise in jar until doubled.

Remove dough from jar and divide into 8 equal lemon-sized balls. Roll dough ball and flatten into a ¼" thick oval shape. Sprinkle one side of rolled dough with water and gently place water side down on a heated griddle. Let it cook for a couple of minutes until it starts to puff and brown on the underside. Flip and cook on the other side until golden brown.

✺ Creating Frozen Treats: Use your Blendtec Blender to make instant and delicious frozen treats. The rapid speed of the blade crushes and smooths frozen ingredients in seconds resulting in a tempting treat.

Peach Frozen Yogurt

Take advantage of seasonal fresh peaches or purchase frozen fruit to make this frozen treat.

FourSide Jar
¾ C low-fat vanilla yogurt
1 small fresh peach, halved and pitted
¼ C honey or agave nectar
2 drops almond extract
16 oz frozen peach slices, approximately 3 C

Add first 4 ingredients to jar and secure lid. Press "Pulse" 6–8 times to blend fresh peach. Add frozen peaches and secure lid. Select "Ice Cream" and serve.

Important Blending Tips

Loading the Jar: For an effortless blend, load your blender jar with liquids first, followed by soft solids and then hard dense items, such as ice and frozen ingredients. Please remember to always secure lid before blending.

Cavitation: When blending extremely thick or cold recipes "cavitation" may occur, where a cavity or air pocket forms above the blade and does not pull food into the blending vortex. Often the solution is to remove the jar from the base, stir the contents and/or increase the liquid in the recipe. To help reduce the possibility of cavitation with thick, cold blends, add banana or avocado in small amounts (i.e. - half a banana or a sliver of avocado). This helps to create more ingredient slippage permitting continual turnover of ingredients through the blades for a smooth blend.

Blend Texture Unsatisfactory: Some ingredients are more solid, dense, thick or more fibrous and may require more blending time. For example, if a smoothie is not completely blended, use the manual controls "Pulse" or "Speed Up" to finish blending. If you reach the desired result before the cycle is complete, press "Stop" or any button to end the cycle. If a smoothie or juice contains excess air and is not silky smooth, try to release air bubbles by pressing "Pulse" 4 times, each time for 1 second. Different ingredients have different blending characteristics. For example when some ingredients are blended they result in a more frothy mixture. Try adding a teaspoon of olive oil, flaxseeds, chia seeds or a sliver of avocado to improve final texture.

Overload: This message on the LCD screen indicates an overload on the motor. Turn off and unplug the machine. Check the blender jar for blockage from ingredients and clear if necessary. Plug in the machine and turn the blender on again to clear the overload condition. Run the motor without the jar as well. If the overload condition re-occurs, please contact your Blendtec customer service representative at 1-800-748-5400.

Overtemperature: This message on the LCD screen is a safeguard to prevent the machine from overheating. Turn off and unplug the machine. Allow it to cool for at least 20 minutes or until the blender cools to operating temperatures.

Frozen Desserts: When making ice cream and other frozen treats in your Blendtec Blender, know that everyone's ice cubes are different. For example, 3 cups of larger ice cubes is equivalent to 2 ½ cups of smaller ice cubes. It may take a few practice cycles to determine how much of your home ice is equivalent to the recipe measurements for that perfect blend. Generally, for those with automatic ice makers at home, the shape of the ice is a crescent or half-moon shaped ice cube. The ice measured in frozen dessert recipes in the book is measured by volume (cups) for convenience. Below is the equivalent of how many ice cubes are in a ½ cup or 1 cup:

    ½ cup ice cubes = 4-5 crescent shaped ice cubes = 2.5 oz ice

    1 cup ice cubes = 8-10 crescent shaped ice cubes = 5 oz ice

After creating your frozen dessert, serve immediately for a soft serve treat or store in the freezer for later. If storing in the freezer, let it soften in the refrigerator for 30–45 minutes before serving. As you begin to create your own soft serve frozen recipes, keep in mind that generally the ratio of liquid to frozen ingredients is 1:2. For example, a frozen dessert recipe with 1 cup liquid (including the sweetener and/or high moisture content foods) generally requires 2 cups frozen ingredients.

Soups: The pre-programmed "Soups" cycle lasts for 90 seconds; this length of time, combined with the speed of the blender, breaks down food ingredients into a smooth soup. When preparing a soup with pre-cooked ingredients, consider selecting a shorter pre-programmed blend cycle (i.e. - "Sauces" or "Smoothie") to prevent excess aeration of the soup. When using fresh ingredients, realize that the speed of blade generates enough heat to warm up fresh produce. Regardless of the temperature of ingredients used when preparing soups, do not add hot liquids or hot ingredients to jar (hot is anything above 115°F).

Whole Juices: The pre-programmed "Whole Juice" cycle lasts 50 seconds. Use the "Whole Juice" cycle if you are using any fruits and/or vegetables with stems, seeds or skins. When preparing carrot juice and other dense fruit and/or vegetable juices, consider repeating the "Whole Juice" cycle once or twice for very fine, smooth, whole juice beverages.

Smoothies: If you would like a thicker smoothie, try adding a few ice cubes, decrease the amount of liquid or if the recipe calls for fresh fruit, freeze the fresh fruit before blending (see page XXVI). If you would like a thinner smoothie, increase the amount of liquid, decrease the amount of ice cubes or use fresh fruit instead of frozen fruit.

Fruit and Vegetable Prep

Preparing Fresh Produce: Blendtec Blenders are capable of blending foods down to the cellular level. The ability to leave on strawberry tops, the kiwi peel, and include the pineapple core allows you to still enjoy a super smooth blend with the added nutritional benefits of fiber, chlorophyll, enzymes, vitamins and minerals.

To Peel or Not to Peel: As a general rule of thumb, if you can easily pierce the skin with your thumbnail, then you can eat it; this test rules out winter squash and bananas but includes tomato, eggplant, and carrot peels. Unless stated otherwise in the recipe, always peel oranges, bananas, kiwis, ginger, avocado, garlic and onion when following recipe instructions. It is important to wash produce thoroughly before consumption to remove surface impurities like wax, soil, bacteria and even some pesticide residues. Under running water, scrub produce with your hands or a small scrub brush. Another option is to put 1 part vinegar and 3 parts water in a spray bottle. Spray enough to cover the fruit and rinse it under the tap. Please remember some foods or elements of food not commonly eaten may naturally contain low-levels of certain toxic compounds, such as cyanogenic acids in apple seeds, which may be harmful to your health. Please use discretion and check with your health or medical professional before consumption.

Mango:

1. Hold mango vertically and cut off mango cheeks.
2. Cut cross-hatch pattern through mango flesh, do not cut through mango skin.
3. Place fingers under mango skin and push flesh upward and outward.
4. Slice off cubed mango flesh by cutting between mango flesh and skin.

Pineapple:

1. Place pineapple on its side and cut off stalk top and bottom.
2. Stand pineapple up again begin slicing off the rind in strips, working your way around the pineapple.
3. Quarter the pineapple into long segments. Remove core or keep the core intact for extra fiber and enzymes.
4. Cut the long segments into pineapple chunks.

Young Coconut:

1. Hold the coconut on its side with one hand. Use a sharp knife, a chef knife or a meat cleaver to shave off the soft white husk until the inner hard brown coconut is exposed.
2. Hold the coconut upright and use the heel of knife to strike the top of the coconut at a 45° angle. Strike the coconut hard enough to crack through the inner shell of the coconut. Work around the top of the coconut striking it a couple more times until you have created a shell lid that lifts open.
3. Lift the shell lid and pour or strain coconut water into a jar for later use in smoothies, frozen desserts or to rehydrate yourself.
4. Wedge a slightly flexible spatula between the brown shell and the tender white coconut meat and work your way around the coconut to remove coconut meat.

Avocado:

1. Grip one side of the avocado in one hand. With a large, sharp knife in the other hand, cut the avocado lengthwise around the pit. Slightly twist the avocado halves to open and expose the pit.

2. To remove the pit, use a spoon to scoop it out or holding the avocado half in a dish towel gently tap the pit with the knife until the knife wedges into the pit. Twist the wedged knife to remove the pit.

3. To remove the avocado flesh, either use a spoon to scoop out flesh or use a small knife to cut the avocado flesh in lengthwise segments or a cross-hatch pattern, then scoop out the flesh.

Freezing Fresh Foods

Buying in bulk can save money and time. As you buy in bulk, it is important to be able to freeze fruit or leafy greens before they spoil. When freezing berries or other fruit, use a technique called IQF (individually quick frozen) to prevent fruit from being frozen into large chunks or blocks. Most fruit can be cut, placed on a sheet tray (to freeze pieces individually), and then stored in an airtight container in the freezer for your next smoothie or frozen dessert.

- For bananas, peel and quarter bananas. Place banana pieces inside a zip-top bag laying flat and freeze until solid.

- For spinach, portion spinach into sandwich size zip-top bags for the perfect portion to add to your next green smoothie.

- For berries or other fruits, place berries or fruit chunks/slices in a single layer on a sheet tray lined with parchment paper. Freeze until solid. Once fruit is completely frozen, transfer them to a resealable freezer bag.

Substitutions and Measurements

Sugar Substitution Chart

The chart below lists general substitutions for granulated sugar, demerara/turbinado sugar and/ or sucanat to honey/agave. The last column is the amount of water to add when substituting sugar for honey/agave nectar.

Using a different sweetener may change both the taste and/or the texture of baked goods. If you want to use honey or agave nectar in a recipe that calls for sugar, start out substituting half the sugar with honey or agave nectar to understand the role it plays in the recipe. Since honey and agave nectar are liquids, with varying viscosities, you will generally need to decrease the liquid in the recipe by ¼ cup to ⅓ cup for each 1 cup of agave or honey used. Decrease baking time slightly and decrease the baking temperature by 25°F.

Note: The recipes containing honey were developed with raw, local honey.

Sugar	Honey/Agave nectar	Approximate Water to Add
1 Tbsp	2 tsp	¾ tsp
¼ C	2 ⅔ Tbsp	1 Tbsp
½ C	⅓ C	2 Tbsp
1 C	⅔ C	¼ C

Ingredient Substitution Chart

	Measurement	Substitution
Allspice	1 tsp	½ teaspoon ground cinnamon plus ½ teaspoon ground cloves
Apple Pie Spice	1 tsp	½ teaspoon ground cinnamon, ¼ teaspoon ground nutmeg, and ⅛ teaspoon ground cardamom
Baking Powder	1 tsp	¼ teaspoon baking soda plus ½ teaspoon cream of tartar
Balsamic Vinegar	1 Tbsp	1 tablespoon cooking sherry or cider vinegar
Broth – Chicken, Beef, or Vegetable	1 C	1 teaspoon chicken, beef, or vegetable bouillon dissolved in 1 cup boiling water.
Brown Sugar	1 C	1 cup granulated sugar plus 2 tablespoons molasses
Butter/Margarine	1 C	1 C hard shortening or ⅞ cup vegetable oil
Buttermilk	1 C	1 tablespoon vinegar or lemon juice plus milk to make 1 cup. Let stand for 5 minutes before use.
Corn Syrup	1 C	1 cup granulated sugar plus ¼ cup water
Cornstarch (for thickening)	1 Tbsp	2 tablespoons all-purpose flour
Dry Mustard	1 tsp	1 tablespoon prepared mustard
Garlic	1 clove	⅛ teaspoon garlic powder or minced dried garlic
Half & Half	1 C	⅞ cup milk plus 3 tablespoons butter
Honey	1 C	1 ¼ cups sugar plus ¼ cup additional liquid plus ½ teaspoon cream of tartar
Leeks	½ C	½ cup sliced shallots or green onions
Milk	1 C	⅓ cup powdered milk plus ⅞ cup water
Molasses	1 C	1 cup honey
Onion	Small bulb	1 teaspoon onion powder

Powdered Sugar	1 C	1 cup sugar plus 1 tablespoon cornstarch; combine and process in blender.
Pumpkin Pie Spice	1 tsp	½ teaspoon ground cinnamon, ¼ teaspoon ground ginger, ⅛ teaspoon ground allspice and ⅛ teaspoon ground nutmeg
Skim Milk	1 C	⅓ cup nonfat dry milk plus ¾ cup water
Sour Cream	1 C	1 cup plain yogurt
Sweetened Condensed Milk	1 C	1 cup nonfat dry milk, ½ cup warm water; mix together and add ¾ cup sugar.
Tomato Juice	1 C	½ cup tomato sauce plus ½ cup water
Tomato Sauce	2 C	¾ cup tomato paste plus 1 cup water
Whole Milk	1 C	½ cup evaporated milk plus ½ cup water

Measurements

Cup	Fluid Ounces	Tablespoon	Teaspoon	Metric (liquid)
1 C	8 fl oz	16 Tbsp	48 tsp	240 mL
¾ C	6 fl oz	12 Tbsp	36 tsp	180 mL·
½ C	4 fl oz	8 Tbsp	24 tsp	120 mL
¼ C	2 fl oz	4 Tbsp	12 tsp	60 mL
⅛ C	1 fl oz	2 Tbsp	6 tsp	30 mL
1/16 C	½ fl oz	1 Tbsp	3 tsp	15 mL
			1 tsp	5 mL

Measurement	Abbreviation
teaspoon	tsp
tablespoon	Tbsp
ounce	oz
fluid ounce	fl oz
pound	lb
liter	L

Classification Icon Key

Each of the recipes in the book are classified according to the following criteria:

Living: The recipe calls for whole food ingredients that require no cooking or heating above a threshold temperature of 113–118°F.

Vegan: The recipe calls for only plant food and no animal products.

Fiber: A serving of the recipe offers 3 grams of fiber or more. Fiber is essential for a healthy diet. Fiber helps absorb cholesterol and reduce the risk of heart disease, diabetes and many kinds of cancer. Fiber also slows down the digestive process and helps you feel full longer, helping to keep the weight off. Simply by eating food naturally rich in fiber, you are simultaneously consuming foods chock full of antioxidants, phytonutrients and lignans, instantly upgrading your diet. The daily recommended amount of fiber is 21–38 g, dependent upon age and gender. Yet most Americans do not even meet half of the daily requirement. To get more fiber, try starting your day off with a green smoothie since many green smoothies contain at least 10 g fiber per serving. Be sure to snack smart and munch on fruits, vegetables, nuts and legumes. Also, remember to choose whole grains over refined grains as often as possible.

Gluten Free: The recipe is gluten-free unless an ingredient added contains gluten. For those with gluten allergies, please always read the label and do not consume foods that contain questionable ingredients unless you can verify they do not contain gluten or are not derived from prohibited grains. If in doubt, go without. Always check the ingredient list and verify ingredients by calling or writing a food manufacturer and specifying the ingredient and the lot number of the food in question.

Low-Sodium: A serving of the recipe contains 140 mg or less of sodium. The recommended maximum intake for sodium is 2,300 mg or about 1 teaspoon of table salt per day. Many people consume more than twice the maximum allowance and most of their sodium consumption comes from packaged and processed foods; take note on food labels and tally up the amount of sodium you consume. Choose low-sodium options whenever possible and make your own sauces, salad dressings and soups in your Blendtec Blender to control the amount of sodium you consume.

Dairy Free: The recipe is lactose-free and casein-free.

Blendtec Favorites: During the development of "Fresh Blends", our team members taste tested and listed these recipes as some of their favorites.

Double WildSide: The double WildSide icon signifies the recipe can be doubled and made in the WildSide jar. Otherwise please prepare the recipe with the jar listed and do not double or triple the recipe.

Beverages

Smoothies

StrawBana Smoothie

A simple smoothie with banana and strawberries that go together so well. Strawberries, the only fruit that wears its seeds on the outside, are an excellent source of Vitamin C and a good source of fiber. Feel free to add a little flaxseed oil to give this smoothie an omega-3 boost.

FourSide Jar

1 C apple juice
1 banana
1 C frozen strawberries

Add ingredients to jar in order listed and secure lid. Select "Smoothie" and serve.

For a workout smoothie, replace the apple juice with soy or almond milk and add a scoop of your preferred protein powder.

Servings 2
Serving Size 12 fl oz
Calories 160
Fat 0 g
Saturated Fat 0 g
Cholesterol 0 mg
Sodium 5 mg
Carbohydrates 41 g
Fiber 5 g
Sugar 27 g
Protein 1 g

Berry Banana Blast

Blueberries are plump with powerful polyphenol compounds acting as antioxidants that neutralize free radicals with a high Oxygen Radical Absorbance Capacity, or ORAC, value. This brain berry has been shown to improve cognitive function.

FourSide Jar

½ C vanilla yogurt
¾ C apple juice
1 banana
¾ C frozen blueberries
1 ½ C frozen strawberries

Add ingredients to jar in order listed and secure lid. Select "Smoothie" and serve.

Servings 2
Serving Size 14 fl oz
Calories 220
Fat 1.5 g
Saturated Fat .5 g
Cholesterol < 5 mg
Sodium 50 mg
Carbohydrates 50 g
Fiber 5 g
Sugar 36 g
Protein 4 g

Tropical Breeze

Servings 2
Serving Size 16 fl oz
Calories 270
Fat 9 g
Saturated Fat 7 g
Cholesterol 0 mg
Sodium 25 mg
Carbohydrates 46 g
Fiber 4 g
Sugar 31 g
Protein 2 g

A refreshing smoothie with a piña colada taste that is not too sweet with a little texture from the shredded coconut.

FourSide Jar

1 C pineapple juice
¼ C coconut milk
2 bananas
2 Tbsp shredded coconut
2 C ice cubes

Add ingredients to jar in order listed and secure lid. Select "Ice Crush" and serve.

Banana Cherry Smoothie

Servings 2
Serving Size 10 fl oz
Calories 200
Fat 1.5 g
Saturated Fat 1 g
Cholesterol < 5 mg
Sodium 60 mg
Carbohydrates 43 g
Fiber 4 g
Sugar 33 g
Protein 6 g

The taste and flavor of this smoothie is slightly reminiscent of cherry pie yogurt. Try serving granola atop the smoothie for a little crunch.

FourSide Jar

¾ C low-fat vanilla yogurt
1 banana
1 ½ C frozen dark sweet cherries
½ C ice cubes

Add ingredients to jar in order listed and secure lid. Select "Ice Crush" and serve.

Strawberry Ginger Refresher

Servings 2
Serving Size 15 fl oz
Calories 170
Fat .5 g
Saturated Fat 0 g
Cholesterol 0 mg
Sodium 5 mg
Carbohydrates 43 g
Fiber 5 g
Sugar 27 g
Protein 2 g

A citrus strawberry smoothie with a mildly inviting undercurrent flavor of fresh ginger.

FourSide Jar

1 ¼ C orange juice
1 banana
1 chunk ginger root, peeled, approximately ½ tsp
2 C frozen strawberries

Add ingredients to jar in order listed and secure lid. Select "Smoothie" and serve.

Orange Carrot Smoothie

As a naturally sweet root, carrots combine perfectly with pineapple and mango to give you a vitamin C and beta-carotene boost at breakfast.

FourSide Jar

¾ C Carrot Juice, see page 17
1 medium orange
¾ C frozen mango chunks
¾ C frozen pineapple chunks

Add ingredients to jar in order listed and secure lid. Select "Smoothie" and serve.

Try adding ½ cup low-fat vanilla yogurt to get a little protein and probiotics (this variation makes the recipe not dairy free).

Servings 2
Serving Size 11 fl oz
Calories 120
Fat 0 g
Saturated Fat 0 g
Cholesterol 0 mg
Sodium 20 mg
Carbohydrates 32 g
Fiber 5 g
Sugar 25 g
Protein 2 g

Spirulina Surge

Known for its health benefits from improving cholesterol to lowering blood pressure, spirulina is a blue green alga rich in vitamins and minerals used as a dietary supplement or whole food.

FourSide Jar

1 C apple juice
½ Tbsp spirulina powder
1 banana
1 C frozen blueberries
¾ C ice cubes

Add ingredients to jar in order listed and secure lid. Select "Ice Crush" and serve.

Servings 2
Serving Size 12 fl oz
Calories 150
Fat 1 g
Saturated Fat 0 g
Cholesterol 0 mg
Sodium 30 mg
Carbohydrates 37 g
Fiber 4 g
Sugar 26 g
Protein 2 g

Berried Up to Here

A very berry blend of strawberries, raspberries, and blueberries that is perfectly sweet and rich in antioxidants. Bite for bite, berries offer a higher concentration of antioxidants than most other foods.

FourSide Jar **2x**

1 ¼ C apple juice
1 C frozen strawberries
½ C frozen raspberries
½ C frozen blueberries

Add ingredients to jar in order listed and secure lid. Select "Smoothie" and serve.

Servings 2
Serving Size 11 fl oz
Calories 150
Fat .5 g
Saturated Fat 0 g
Cholesterol 0 mg
Sodium 10 mg
Carbohydrates 36 g
Fiber 7 g
Sugar 27 g
Protein 1 g

Protein Power Crunch

Whether you're needing some protein and carbs after the gym or are looking for a meal replacement shake, this recipe will leave you satisfied.

FourSide Jar

¾ C milk
¼ hemp granola
1 banana
1 scoop protein powder, approximately 2 Tbsp of soy, rice, hemp or whey protein
1 C ice cubes

Add ingredients to jar in order listed and secure lid. Select "Ice Crush" and serve.

For a little plant protein and a healthy source of fat, add 1 tablespoon of nuts to the blend.

For a chocolate variation, add ½ tablespoon cocoa powder.

Servings 1
Serving Size 20 fl oz
Calories 450
Fat 9 g
Saturated Fat 4 g
Cholesterol 80 mg
Sodium 190 mg
Carbohydrates 65 g
Fiber 7 g
Sugar 37 g
Protein 32 g

Pumpkin Pleaser

The combo of probiotics, pumpkin and a little protein is a great way to start any day.

WildSide Jar

¾ C orange juice
1 C low-fat vanilla yogurt
1 C pumpkin purée
1 tsp pumpkin pie spice
2 bananas, quartered and frozen
1 C ice cubes

Add ingredients to jar and secure lid. Select "Smoothie" and serve.

For less citrus taste, substitute milk for part or all the orange juice.

For a Cranberry Orange Smoothie, substitute the pumpkin purée and pumpkin pie spice for 1 cup cranberries and 1 tsp vanilla extract.

Servings 3
Serving Size 12 fl oz
Calories 200
Fat 1.5 g
Saturated Fat 1 g
Cholesterol < 5 mg
Sodium 60 mg
Carbohydrates 43 g
Fiber 5 g
Sugar 29 g
Protein 6 g

Go Man-Go

Get up and going in the morning with your dose of vitamin C in this nice thick smoothie. It's easy to double this recipe for a larger crowd.

FourSide Jar

½ C mango nectar
½ C orange juice
½ banana
1 C frozen mango chunks
2 frozen strawberries

Add ingredients to jar in order listed and secure lid. Select "Ice Crush" and serve.

Servings 2
Serving Size 10 fl oz
Calories 160
Fat 0 g
Saturated Fat 0 g
Cholesterol 0 mg
Sodium 0 mg
Carbohydrates 39 g
Fiber 3 g
Sugar 32 g
Protein 2 g

Sunny Side Up

A delicious morning smoothie flavored to match the color of the sunrise.

FourSide Jar

1 ½ C orange juice
1 banana
2 Tbsp wheat germ
1 C frozen mango chunks
1 C frozen pineapple chunks

Add ingredients to jar in order listed and secure lid. Select "Smoothie" and serve.

Servings 2
Serving Size 14 fl oz
Calories 270
Fat 1.5 g
Saturated Fat 0 g
Cholesterol 0 mg
Sodium 0 mg
Carbohydrates 65 g
Fiber 6 g
Sugar 47 g
Protein 4 g

Chocolate Peanut Butter Smoothie

A smoothie great for breakfast fuel or suited to satisfy a chocolate craving in the afternoon.

FourSide Jar

½ C milk
1 ½ Tbsp peanut butter
1 Tbsp honey
½ Tbsp cocoa powder
1 banana
1 C ice cubes

Add ingredients to jar in order listed and secure lid. Select "Sauces" and serve.

Servings 1
Serving Size 16 fl oz
Calories 360
Fat 13 g
Saturated Fat 3 g
Cholesterol < 5 mg
Sodium 160 mg
Carbohydrates 56 g
Fiber 5 g
Sugar 40 g
Protein 12 g

Papaya Passion

Servings 2
Serving Size 12 fl oz
Calories 170
Fat 0 g
Saturated Fat 0 g
Cholesterol 0 mg
Sodium 5 mg
Carbohydrates 41 g
Fiber 3 g
Sugar 31 g
Protein < 1 g

Papaya is an excellent source of vitamin C and this buttery, bright orange fruit's claim to fame is papain, an important enzyme. Papayas are picked green and will ripen at room temperature. They're ready to eat when the skin is an orange to yellow hue and yields slightly to the touch, like a pear.

FourSide Jar

1 C mango nectar
1 C papaya chunks
1 Tbsp fresh lime juice
¾ C frozen pineapple chunks
½ banana, halved and frozen
½ C ice cubes

Add ingredients to jar in order listed and secure lid. Select "Ice Crush" and serve.

Acaí Berry Smoothie

Servings 2
Serving Size 11 fl oz
Calories 170
Fat 3.5 g
Saturated Fat 1 g
Cholesterol < 5 mg
Sodium 50 mg
Carbohydrates 33 g
Fiber 3 g
Sugar 28 g
Protein 4 g

Touted as a superfood and ranked as one of the best foods to scavenge for free radicals in your body, acaí can be found in the frozen food section in your local health food store.

FourSide Jar

¾ C pomegranate juice
½ C low-fat vanilla yogurt
¾ C frozen blueberries
½ C ice cubes
3.5 oz frozen pouch acaí purée

Add ingredients to jar in order listed and secure lid. Select "Smoothie" and serve.

Green Smoothies

Berry Banana

Servings 1
Serving Size 18 fl oz
Calories 200
Fat 1 g
Saturated Fat 0 g
Cholesterol 0 mg
Sodium 95 mg
Carbohydrates 49 g
Fiber 11 g
Sugar 24 g
Protein 5 g

The combinations are limitless when it comes to green smoothies. You can taste the blueberries and banana in this not-so green, green smoothie.

FourSide Jar

¾ C water
1 banana
2 C spinach
1 C frozen blueberries

Add ingredients to jar in order listed and secure lid. Select "Smoothie" and serve.

Greeña Colada

Servings 4
Serving Size 12 fl oz
Calories 180
Fat 3.5 g
Saturated Fat 3 g
Cholesterol 0 mg
Sodium 25 mg
Carbohydrates 38 g
Fiber 4 g
Sugar 26 g
Protein 2 g

A perfect summer sipper by the pool that is hydrating and super refreshing. No one will taste the spinach.

WildSide Jar

1 young coconut, approximately 1½ C coconut water and ½ C coconut meat
3 ½ C pineapple chunks, chilled
1 lime, peeled
2 C spinach
½ tsp vanilla extract
3 Tbsp agave nectar
1 C ice cubes

Open young coconut, scrape meat and add coconut water and meat to jar. Add remaining ingredients in order listed and secure lid. Select "Smoothie" and serve.

Vitamins C and E have the ability to prevent and repair cellular damage caused by UV radiation. On a day you'll be out in the sun, get these vitamins in your system to fortify your skin. Drink this smoothie, rich in vitamin A and C, and grab an ounce, or small handful, of almonds or sunflower seeds to obtain nearly half of your recommended Vitamin E intake.

Green Mango Madness

With two servings of fruit and one serving of veggies, this smoothie makes for a great mid-day snack. For a well-rounded breakfast, add some protein to the smoothie or grab a handful of nut granola to snack on.

Servings 1
Serving Size 22 fl oz
Calories 220
Fat 0.5 g
Saturated Fat 0 g
Cholesterol 0 mg
Sodium 95 mg
Carbohydrates 55 g
Fiber 10 g
Sugar 43 g
Protein 5 g

Either Jar
¾ C water
1 orange
1 ripe mango, peeled and cubed
2 C spinach
½ C ice cubes

Add ingredients to jar in order listed and secure lid. Select "Smoothie" and serve.

Tropical Sea Breeze

A slightly sweet and delicious way to add some lovely green leafies to your day and share with others. Kiwis are nutrient dense, green gems containing almost twice as much vitamin C as oranges and nearly the same amount of potassium as a banana of equal weight.

Servings 3
Serving Size 12 fl oz
Calories 130
Fat 0 g
Saturated Fat 0 g
Cholesterol 0 mg
Sodium 80 mg
Carbohydrates 30 g
Fiber 4 g
Sugar 13 g
Protein 4 g

WildSide Jar
1 ½ C coconut water
2 kiwis, peeled
3 C spinach
1 Tbsp spirulina powder
1 C frozen pineapple chunks
1 banana, quartered and frozen

Add ingredients to jar in order listed and secure lid. Select "Smoothie" and serve.

Green Flaxy

A great way to improve your omega-6 to omega-3 ratio is to enjoy this smoothie containing 1.5 grams of omega-3 fatty acids.

Servings 2
Serving Size 10 fl oz
Calories 180
Fat 4 g
Saturated Fat 0 g
Cholesterol 0 mg
Sodium 50 mg
Carbohydrates 35 g
Fiber 8 g
Sugar 18 g
Protein 5 g

FourSide Jar
½ C water
2 Tbsp flaxseeds
2 clementines, peeled
1 banana
2 C spinach
½ C frozen pineapple chunks

Add all ingredients to jar in order listed and secure lid. Select "Whole Juice" and serve.

Peaches and Cream Green

A creamy green start to any morning, helping you get your daily dose of vitamin A and C.

Servings 2
Serving Size 14 fl oz
Calories 140
Fat 2 g
Saturated Fat 0 g
Cholesterol 0 mg
Sodium 60 mg
Carbohydrates 26 g
Fiber 6 g
Sugar 13 g
Protein 7 g

FourSide Jar
1 C almond milk
1 banana
2 C spinach
1 ¼ C frozen peach slices

Add the ingredients to jar in order listed and secure lid. Select "Ice Crush" and serve.

Green Pineapple Paradise

Half of an alligator pear, aka avocado, offers a rich creaminess to this satisfying smoothie.

Servings 1
Serving Size 22 fl oz
Calories 290
Fat 11 g
Saturated Fat 1.5 g
Cholesterol 0 mg
Sodium 100 mg
Carbohydrates 50 g
Fiber 12 g
Sugar 31 g
Protein 6 g

FourSide Jar
¾ C water
2 C pineapple chunks
½ medium ripe avocado, peeled and pitted
2 C spinach
½ C ice cubes

Add ingredients to jar in order listed and secure lid. Select "Smoothie" and serve.

Green-AC Booster

With a triple daily dose of vitamin A and C, this simple summer green smoothie is great for green smoothie beginners.

Servings 1
Serving Size 20 fl oz
Calories 200
Fat 1 g
Saturated Fat 0 g
Cholesterol 0 mg
Sodium 140 mg
Carbohydrates 46 g
Fiber 9 g
Sugar 37 g
Protein 7 g

FourSide Jar
2 C cantaloupe chunks
1 orange
2 C spinach
½ C ice cubes

Add ingredients to jar in order listed and secure lid. Select "Smoothie" and serve.

Juices

Carrot Juice

A quick way to get your daily dose of vitamin A with fiber.

Servings 7
Serving Size 4 fl oz
Calories 15
Fat 0 g
Saturated Fat 0 g
Cholesterol 0 mg
Sodium 25 mg
Carbohydrates 4 g
Fiber <1 g
Sugar 2 g
Protein 0 g

Either Jar
2 C water
2 C carrots, roughly chopped, approximately 3 lg carrots
1 Tbsp fresh lemon juice
1 tsp ginger root, peeled
¾ C ice

Add ingredients to jar in order listed and secure lid. Select "Whole Juice" and serve.

Berry Grape Juice

A delicious whole juice with a little body that adds nutrition by keeping the pulp that most juicers remove.

Servings 2
Serving Size 8 fl oz
Calories 130
Fat 0 g
Saturated Fat 0 g
Cholesterol 0 mg
Sodium 0 mg
Carbohydrates 33 g
Fiber 3 g
Sugar 27 g
Protein 2 g

FourSide Jar
2 C red grapes
1 C strawberries

Add ingredients to jar in order listed and secure lid. Select "Whole Juice" and serve.

Pineapple Juice

Pineapple juice blended up with a little body and bromelain. Bromelain, found in the pineapple's core and stem, is used commercially as a meat tenderizer but is marked for it's therapeutic use as a natural anti-imflammatory and digestive enzyme aid.

Servings 4
Serving Size 8 fl oz
Calories 75
Fat 0 g
Saturated Fat 0 g
Cholesterol 0 mg
Sodium 0 mg
Carbohydrates 19 g
Fiber 3 g
Sugar 13 g
Protein < 1 g

Either Jar
3 ½ cups pineapple chunks
1 C ice cubes

Add ingredients to jar and secure lid. Select "Whole Juice" and serve.

Tomato Vegetable Juice

A low-sodium, fresh, tomato vegetable juice to enjoy morning, noon or night.

Servings 2
Serving Size 8 fl oz
Calories 40
Fat 0 g
Saturated Fat 0 g
Cholesterol 0 mg
Sodium 80 mg
Carbohydrates 8 g
Fiber 3 g
Sugar 5 g
Protein 2 g

FourSide Jar
½ C water
2 Roma tomatoes
½ stalk celery
2" slice red bell pepper
½ green onion
⅛" slice lemon
¹⁄₁₆ tsp kosher salt
8 drops Worcestershire sauce

Add ingredients to jar in order listed and secure lid. Select "Whole Juice" and serve.

Try replacing water with low-sodium tomato juice for a more intense red color and tomato flavor.

For those with gluten allergies, please ensure the Worcestershire sauce is gluten-free.

Milk Alternatives

Coconut Milk

Nothing can compare with the subtleties of fresh coconut milk.

Note: Nutritional
information is not
given due to
variation in amount
of water added.
Most commercial
varieties contain
110 calories and
12 g fat per ¼ cup
serving.

Either Jar
1 mature coconut, drained, cracked and meat removed
4 C water

First, empty coconut water by carefully taking a small knife and try pushing in each eye of the coconut until you find the soft eye. Drain coconut water coming from the soft eye into a bowl and set aside for future use in a smoothie or when blending the coconut meat.

Take mature coconut in one hand and a knife, or hammer, in the opposite. Carefully hit the coconut using the blunt edge of knife along its natural fault line between the two tips of the coconut. Continue hitting and turning the coconut along its fault line until it is cracked open.

To remove meat, either use a hand-held coconut grater, seated or countertop grater, or soak coconut halves in water for 5–10 minutes and use a knife to wedge between meat and shell to separate them.

Rinse coconut meat pieces with water. Add 2 cups of water and half of coconut meat to jar and secure lid. Select "Whole Juice". Pour contents into a mesh strainer lined with muslin cloth to strain. Allow the milk to drain for a few minutes then gather ends of cloth and squeeze the cloth to extract as much liquid as possible. Repeat process with the other half of coconut meat.

Note: By adjusting the amount of water added to blender and by cooking, you can control the thickness and consistency of coconut milk. Store in refrigerator for 1–2 days. Without adding an emulsifier and thickener such as guar gum, the milk separates after sitting and will need to be reblended.

Rather than cracking a fresh coconut, you can buy unsweetened shredded coconut chips. Soak 1 ½ cups unsweetened shredded coconut chips in 3 cups water. Transfer soaking water and coconut to FourSide or WildSide jar and secure lid. Select "Whole Juice". Pour contents into a mesh strainer lined with muslin cloth to strain.

Almond Milk

Almond milk is great for cereals, desserts and savory-sweet dishes. Almonds are an alkaline nut and one serving helps you get ⅓ of your daily dose of vitamin E.

Note: Nutritional information is not given due to variation of pulp removal. Most unsweetened commercial varieties of almond milk contain 40 calories and 3 g fat per cup serving.

Either Jar
4 C water
1 C almonds, soaked overnight and rinsed
2 Tbsp agave nectar
1 tsp vanilla extract or vanilla seeds scraped from bean
⅛ tsp kosher salt

Add ingredients to jar in order listed and secure lid. Select "Whole Juice". Strain milk through nut milk bag or cheesecloth to remove almond skins and pulp. Rinse blender jar and place strained almond milk back in jar with remaining ingredients. Secure lid and press "Pulse" 3–5 times to combine thoroughly. Serve or store in refrigerator for up to 3 days.

Keep the almond pulp and dehydrate it to use as defatted almond meal in other recipes.

Cashew Milk

Cashew milk, well blended, needs no straining and tastes great in smoothies, baked items or cereal.

Servings 4
Serving Size 8 fl oz
Calories 190
Fat 14 g
Saturated Fat 2.5 g
Cholesterol 0 mg
Sodium 35 mg
Carbohydrates 14 g
Fiber 1 g
Sugar 6 g
Protein 6 g

Either Jar
1 C cashews, soaked overnight and rinsed
4 C water
1 Tbsp agave nectar

Add ingredients to jar in order listed and secure lid. Select "Whole Juice". Serve or store in refrigerator for up to 3 days.

Depending on personal preference, use more or less water to vary the thickness of your raw cashew milk. A 4:1 ratio of water to cashews is similar to whole milk in taste. If you add another cup of water, the resulting 5:1 ratio is similar to 2% milk.

Hemp Milk

A rich and nutty flavor similar to that of sunflower seeds, hemp seeds provide an appropriate 3:1 ratio of omega-6 to omega-3 fatty acids. Hemp also contains all the essential amino acids that our body does not make and must get from our diet.

Either Jar

¾ C hemp seeds
4 C water
2 Tbsp agave nectar
⅛ tsp kosher salt

Add ingredients to jar in order listed and secure lid. Select "Whole Juice". For commercial style hemp milk, strain milk through nut milk bag or cheesecloth to remove pulp. Serve or store in refrigerator for up to 3 days.

Note: Nutritional information is not given but most commercial varieties contain 110 calories and 7 g fat per cup serving.

Soy Milk

In five steps of soaking, heating, straining, boiling and flavoring, you'll have okara and homemade soy milk to enjoy.

WildSide Jar

¾ C dry soybeans, soaked overnight and rinsed
4 ½ C water

Take soaked soy beans and remove soybean hulls by kneading the soybeans in soaking water. Flush the loose hulls off in running water. Heat the soybeans for a couple minutes by microwaving or steaming to reduce enzyme activity and reduce bean flavor. Add soybeans and 4 ½ cups water to jar and secure lid. Select "Soups". Strain mixture through cheesecloth and fine mesh sieve over large pot. Bring soy milk to boil and simmer 5–10 minutes. Add desired flavorings such as honey, maple syrup, vanilla, and a pinch of salt. Cool and store in refrigerator for up to 3 days.

Keep the okara, or soy pulp, which is packed with protein and filled with fiber for the next batch of breakfast muffins, okara chocolate cake or okara seitan.

For a quick soy milk variation, add 2 cups warm water and ⅓ cup dry soy beans to jar and secure lid. Run the "Soup" cycle twice. Add spice or sweetener to taste, such as agave nectar, vanilla, cocoa or cinnamon. Note: Let milk settle for 5–10 minutes in order to separate and skim off foam.

Note: Nutritional information is not given but most unsweetened commercial varieties of soy milk contain 80 calories and 4 g fat per cup serving.

Coffee

Chinese Chill

A sweet and bold coffee drink with five spice powder that lifts the coffee flavor. Common in Asian cuisine, five spice powder is combination of five spices varying from anise to fennel seeds. Find it in the spice aisle at a well-stocked grocery store or at a local Asian market.

FourSide Jar

⅓ C low-fat milk
¼ C low-fat sweetened condensed milk
⅔ C vanilla ice cream
2 Tbsp instant coffee granules
½ tsp Chinese five spice
½ C ice cubes

Add ingredients to jar in order listed and secure lid. Select "Milkshake" and serve.

For any leftover sweetened condensed milk, pour into a resalable container and store it in the refrigerator or freezer. You can add a spoonful to your coffee or hot chocolate, add it to your morning oatmeal with cinnamon, use it in rice pudding or try adding a little to sweeten your smoothies.

Servings 2
Serving Size 6 fl oz
Calories 260
Fat 8 g
Saturated Fat 4.5 g
Cholesterol 30 mg
Sodium 105 mg
Carbohydrates 39 g
Fiber 0 g
Sugar 36 g
Protein 7 g

Cappuccino Cooler

A slightly sweet, frozen blended coffee; perfectly suited for adding your favorite extract or syrup.

FourSide Jar

¾ C double-strength coffee
¼ C milk
3 ½ Tbsp agave nectar
2 C ice cubes

Add ingredients to jar in order listed and secure lid. Select "Sauces" and serve.

Servings 3
Serving Size 9 fl oz
Calories 80
Fat 0 g
Saturated Fat 0 g
Cholesterol 0 mg
Sodium 10 mg
Carbohydrates 20 g
Fiber 0 g
Sugar 20 g
Protein < 1 g

Mocha Frappé

A light and delicious way to get your coffee fix in the morning, or for sharing with your friends on the weekend without the $5 price tag. Make extra coffee cubes and keep them on hand stored in the freezer in a zip-top bag.

Servings 4
Serving Size 12 fl oz
Calories 150
Fat 2 g
Saturated Fat 1 g
Cholesterol < 5 mg
Sodium 100 mg
Carbohydrates 28 g
Fiber 1 g
Sugar 25 g
Protein 7 g

WildSide Jar
2 C double-strength coffee, frozen into ice cubes
2 ¼ C milk
¼ C agave nectar
¼ C chocolate syrup

Pour 2 cups of chilled, strong brewed coffee into an ice cube tray and freeze for 2–3 hours or until solid. Add milk, agave nectar, chocolate syrup, and coffee ice cubes to jar and secure lid. Select "Ice Crush" and serve.

For an extra special treat, serve with a dollop of whipped cream and chocolate shavings.

Alcohol

Island Lei

A tangy tropical treat with a lively splash of fruit flavors.

Either Jar
4 fl oz light rum
¾ C grapefruit juice
¾ C orange juice
2 bananas
2 C ice cubes

Add ingredients to jar in order listed and secure lid. Select "Ice Crush" and serve.

For a non-alcoholic version, substitute the rum with white grape or apple juice. Try freezing the bananas and omit ice for a thicker tropical treat.

Strawberry Daiquiri

Top this drink off with a little whipped cream to sweeten each sip.

FourSide Jar 2x
4 fl oz light rum
2 Tbsp fresh lime juice
2 Tbsp agave nectar
1 ½ C frozen strawberries
¼ C ice cubes

Add ingredients to jar in order listed and secure lid. Select "Ice Crush" and serve.

Frozen Screwdriver

This is a twist on the traditional Screwdriver, tasting like a creamsicle with a kick.

Either Jar
4 fl oz vodka
1 ½ C orange juice
1 Tbsp agave nectar
1 C reduced fat vanilla ice cream
1 ½ C ice cubes

Add ingredients to jar in order listed and secure lid. Select "Sauces" and serve.

Piña Colada

Servings 3
Serving Size 9 fl oz
Calories 250
Fat 9 g
Saturated Fat 7 g
Cholesterol 0 mg
Sodium 5 mg
Carbohydrates 27 g
Fiber 1 g
Sugar 24 g
Protein 1 g

A tropical treat with plenty of fresh pineapple. Depending on the rum, you may want to up the alcohol or tone it down.

Either Jar
3 fl oz light rum
⅓ C coconut milk
3 Tbsp agave nectar
1 ½ C pineapple chunks
2 C ice cubes

Add ingredients to jar in order listed and secure lid. Select "Ice Crush" and serve.

Adult Espresso Milkshake

Servings 4
Serving Size 12 fl oz
Calories 330
Fat 14 g
Saturated Fat 9 g
Cholesterol 75 mg
Sodium 90 mg
Carbohydrates 28 g
Fiber 0 g
Sugar 27 g
Protein 5 g

A rich and fluid frozen dessert that offers a little more than a pick me up.

WildSide Jar
¾ C double strength coffee, chilled
1 C low-fat milk
3 fl oz coffee liqueur
2 fl oz vodka
1 ½ C vanilla ice cream
2 C ice cubes

Add ingredients to jar in order listed and secure lid. Select "Ice Crush" and serve.

Frozen Mojito

Serve this refreshing drink next time you're making a Tex-Mex dinner.

Servings 3
Serving Size 6 fl oz
Calories 170
Fat 0 g
Saturated Fat 0 g
Cholesterol 0 mg
Sodium 0 mg
Carbohydrates 23 g
Fiber 0 g
Sugar 22 g
Protein 0 g

FourSide Jar

4 fl oz light rum
¼ C agave nectar
¼ C fresh lime juice
10–12 mint leaves plus mint sprigs for garnish
2 ½ C ice cubes

Add ingredients to jar in order listed and secure lid. Select "Ice Crush" and serve.

Frozen Margarita

Servings 2
Serving Size 11 fl oz
Calories 270
Fat 0 g
Saturated Fat 0 g
Cholesterol 0 mg
Sodium 5 mg
Carbohydrates 40 g
Fiber 0 g
Sugar 38 g
Protein 0 g

A basic frozen margarita blend, great for a warm summer afternoon. Fresh-squeezed lime juice beats canned frozen limeade anytime.

FourSide Jar
¼ C fresh lime juice
¼ C agave nectar
3 fl oz tequila
1 fl oz triple sec
2 ½ C ice cubes

Add ingredients to jar in order listed and secure lid. Select "Sauces" and serve.

Frosted Cosmo

Servings 4
Serving Size 7 fl oz
Calories 190
Fat 0 g
Saturated Fat 0 g
Cholesterol 0 mg
Sodium 0 mg
Carbohydrates 26 g
Fiber 0 g
Sugar 25 g
Protein 0 g

A tart and fresh beverage for a night with the ladies.

FourSide Jar
½ C cranberry juice
4 fl oz vodka
2 fl oz triple sec
¼ C agave nectar
2 Tbsp fresh lime juice
2 ½ C ice cubes

Add ingredients to jar in order listed and secure lid. Select "Sauces" and serve.

Whiskey Sour Slush

Servings 4
Serving Size 8 fl oz
Calories 200
Fat 0 g
Saturated Fat 0 g
Cholesterol 0 mg
Sodium 0 mg
Carbohydrates 27 g
Fiber < 1 g
Sugar 25 g
Protein 0 g

Your tongue first recognizes the sweet and then the sour taste kicks in gear.

FourSide Jar
6 fl oz bourbon
¼ C fresh lemon juice
⅓ C agave nectar
1 orange
3 C ice cubes

Add ingredients to jar in order listed and secure lid. Select "Sauces" and serve.

Sweet Sips

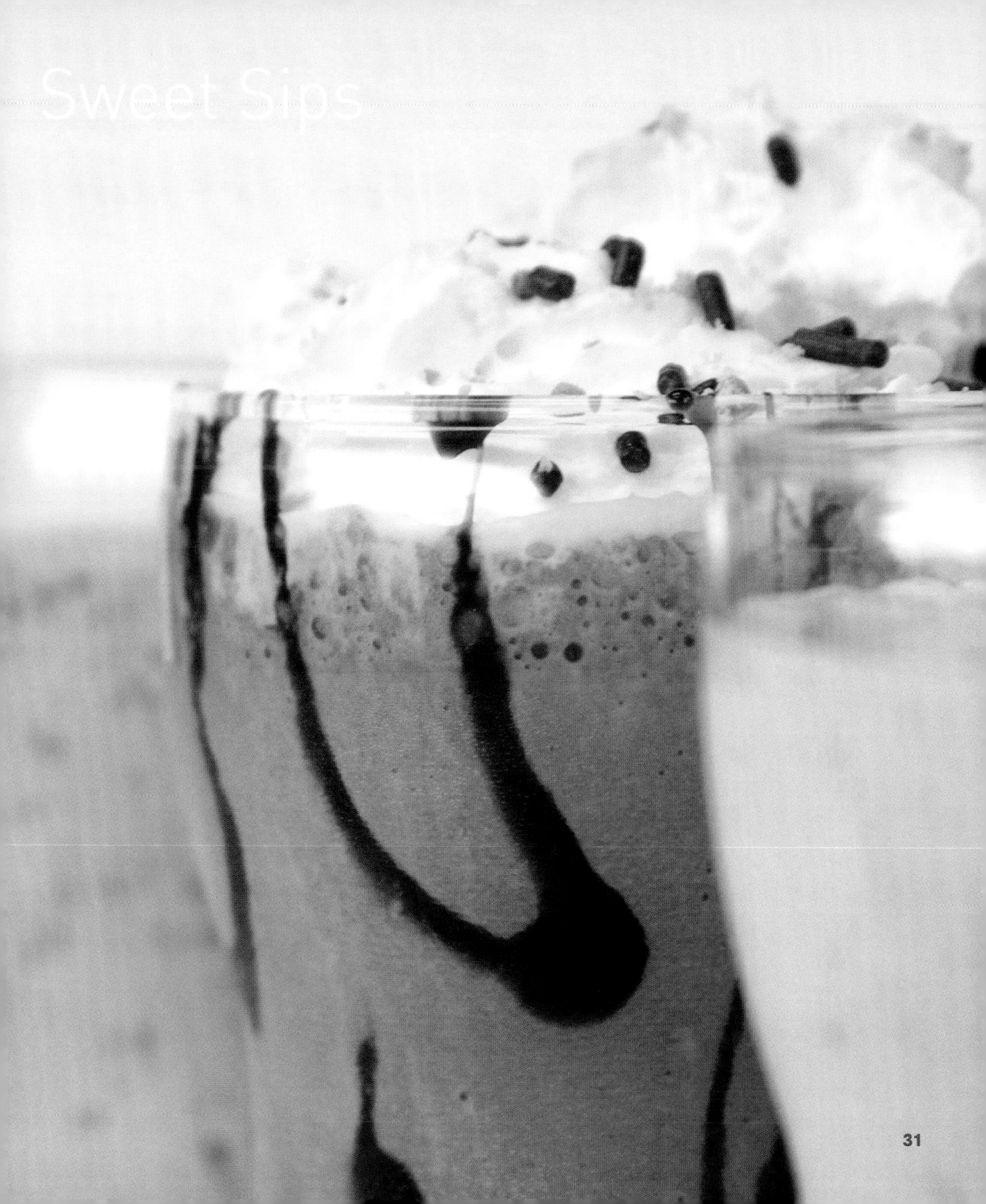

Fudgesicle Frosty

A versatile dessert that can be served as a quick fudgy frosty or frozen to make yummy fudgesicles.

Servings 3
Serving Size 9 fl oz
Calories 330
Fat 15 g
Saturated Fat 11 g
Cholesterol 0 mg
Sodium 12 mg
Carbohydrates 56 g
Fiber 7 g
Sugar 44 g
Protein 4 g

Either Jar
⅔ C coconut milk
¼ C agave nectar
⅓ C cocoa powder
4 Medjool dates, pitted
½ large ripe avocado, peeled and pitted
3 C ice cubes

Add first 5 ingredients to jar and secure lid. Select "Sauces". Add ice cubes to jar and secure lid. Select "Ice Cream" and serve immediately for a frosty treat.

For a full recipe of fudgesicles, substitute 1 cup of ice cubes for 1 cup of plain almond or soy milk. After blending, pour the frosty into popsicle mold, insert popsicle sticks and freeze until solid.

For a recipe with no avocado, use ¾ cup coconut milk, ⅓ cup agave nectar, 3 tablespoon cocoa or carob powder, ½ teaspoon xanthan gum to jar and secure lid. Press "Pulse" 4–5 times until the blend becomes more viscous. Add 3 cups of ice cubes and secure lid. Select "Ice Cream" and serve.

Agua Fresca de Sandia

Aguas Frescas is to Central America as lemonade is to the United States on a warm summer day.

Servings 5
Serving Size 8 fl oz
Calories 65
Fat 0 g
Saturated Fat 0 g
Cholesterol 0 mg
Sodium 4 mg
Carbohydrates 17 g
Fiber 0.5 g
Sugar 15 g
Protein < 1 g

WildSide Jar
2 C water
3 C watermelon, seeded and cubed
3 Tbsp agave nectar
2 Tbsp fresh lime juice

Add ingredients to jar in order listed and secure lid. Press "Speed Up" to Speed 1 for 25 seconds and press "Pulse" to stop cycle. Serve and garnish with lime slices and ice.

Try different fruits or vegetables such as pineapple, strawberries or cucumber.

Mango Lassi

Cool off after eating hot curry with this nutritious and refreshing drink. The casein in dairy helps alleviate the heat of capsaicin in peppers. You can also enjoy this sweet lassi as a light breakfast or as a healthy snack between meals.

Servings 2
Serving Size 10 fl oz
Calories 130
Fat 2 g
Saturated Fat 1 g
Cholesterol 5 mg
Sodium 90 mg
Carbohydrates 23 g
Fiber 2 g
Sugar 21 g
Protein 7 g

FourSide Jar
1 C water
1 C low-fat vanilla yogurt
1 C mango chunks
⅛ tsp ground cardamom

Add ingredients to jar in order listed and secure lid. Select "Sauces" and serve.

Strawberry Lime Slush

A cool and refreshing beverage for a warm day. The lime offers a tart touch to accompany the sweet berries.

FourSide Jar

1 C water
2 limes, peeled
3 Tbsp agave nectar
2 C frozen strawberries

Add ingredients to jar in order listed and secure lid. Select "Whole Juice" and serve.

For a Cherry Lime Slush, follow the instructions above except decrease agave nectar to 2 tablespoons, add 2 cups frozen dark sweet cherries in place of frozen strawberries and add ½ cup ice cubes to jar. Select "Whole Juice" and serve.

Servings 2
Serving Size 12 fl oz
Calories 150
Fat 0 g
Saturated Fat 0 g
Cholesterol 0 mg
Sodium 10 mg
Carbohydrates 41 g
Fiber 3 g
Sugar 33 g
Protein < 1 g

Raspberry Milkshake

Servings 2
Serving Size 8 fl oz
Calories 300
Fat 8 g
Saturated Fat 4 g
Cholesterol 20 mg
Sodium 40 mg
Carbohydrates 48 g
Fiber 2 g
Sugar 45 g
Protein 9 g

Everybody will rave over this raspberry milkshake. Try adding a couple slices of peaches and decreasing milk to ⅓ cup for raspberry peach perfection.

FourSide Jar

½ C low-fat milk
½ C raspberries
1 Tbsp honey
2 C reduced fat vanilla ice cream

Add ingredients to jar in order listed and secure lid. Select "Ice Crush" and serve in chilled glasses.

For Blueberry Milkshake, substitute the ½ cup of raspberries for ½ cup of blueberries and decrease honey to ½ tablespoon.

For Strawberry Milkshake, substitute ½ cup raspberries for 5–6 medium strawberries and decrease milk to ⅓ cup.

For Chocolate Milkshake, omit the honey and raspberries and use ⅓ cup chocolate syrup.

Honey Ginger-Ale

Servings 4
Serving Size 8 fl oz
Calories 140
Fat 0 g
Saturated Fat 0 g
Cholesterol 0 mg
Sodium 10 mg
Carbohydrates 37 g
Fiber 0 g
Sugar 34 g
Protein 0 g

Honey and agave nectar sweeten this fresh ginger-ale.

FourSide Jar

⅓ C ginger root, peeled and roughly chopped
⅓ C fresh lemon juice
¼ C honey
¼ C agave nectar
1 L sparkling water, chilled

Add first 4 ingredients to jar in order listed and secure lid. Select "Whole Juice". Pour blend into mesh strainer lined with cheesecloth and drain. Gather edges of cheesecloth and squeeze firmly to extract as much juice as possible. Pour ¼ cup of blend into each glass and add sparkling water. Serve with ice cubes and fresh lemon slices if desired.

Breakfast and Brunch

Batters

Whole Wheat Pancakes

Servings 6
Serving Size 2 pancakes
Calories 210
Fat 7 g
Saturated Fat 1 g
Cholesterol 70 mg
Sodium 270 mg
Carbohydrates 31 g
Fiber 4 g
Sugar 7 g
Protein 7 g

These wholesome pancakes, also known as pioneer pancakes, are perfectly paired with peach butter and raspberry maple syrup.

FourSide Jar

1 ½ C low-fat milk

1 C wheat berries

2 Tbsp canola oil

2 lg eggs

2 Tbsp granulated sugar

1 Tbsp baking powder

½ tsp kosher salt

Add milk and wheat berries to jar and secure lid. Press "Speed Up" to Speed 9 and run full cycle. Add remaining ingredients to jar and secure lid. Press "Pulse" 5–7 times to incorporate remaining ingredients. Allow batter to rest 5 minutes. Heat griddle or other pan over medium to medium high heat and grease. Pour approximately ¼ cup batter onto heated pan and cook approximately 1 minute or until bubbles break the surface of the pancake and the underside is golden brown. Flip and cook for approximately 30 seconds. Repeat with remaining batter. Serve immediately or keep warm in the oven at 200°F loosely wrapped in foil.

Basic Waffle

A great basic recipe for waffles with a crisp exterior and soft interior.

Servings 9
Serving Size 1 waffle
Calories 200
Fat 8 g
Saturated Fat 4 g
Cholesterol 85 mg
Sodium 350 mg
Carbohydrates 27 g
Fiber 2 g
Sugar 7 g
Protein 7 g

Either Jar

3 lg eggs
¼ C butter, softened
2 C low-fat buttermilk
3 Tbsp granulated sugar
1 tsp baking powder
½ tsp baking soda
¾ tsp kosher salt
1 C all-purpose flour
1 C whole wheat flour

Add eggs and butter to jar and secure lid. Select "Batters". Add remaining ingredients in order listed and secure lid. Press "Pulse" 4–6 times to incorporate ingredients; do not over blend. Allow batter to rest 5 minutes; heat waffle iron to medium high heat. Depending on waffle iron size, pour appropriate amount of batter onto greased iron and cook until golden brown. Repeat with remaining batter.

To cut down on the saturated fat, substitute a mild flavored oil for the butter.

Banana Spelt Pancakes

Servings 4
Serving Size 2 pancakes
Calories 220
Fat 7 g
Saturated Fat 3 g
Cholesterol 0 mg
Sodium 210 mg
Carbohydrates 33 g
Fiber 5 g
Sugar 8 g
Protein 7 g

With a slightly nuttier and sweeter taste, spelt deepens the flavor of this quick breakfast treat.

FourSide Jar

1 C milk
2 Tbsp flaxseeds
1 ripe banana
1 C spelt flour
1 Tbsp sucanat
1 Tbsp coconut oil
1 ½ tsp baking powder
½ tsp ground cinnamon
1 tsp vanilla extract
¼ tsp kosher salt

Add milk and flaxseeds to jar and secure lid. Select "Batters". Add remaining ingredients to jar in order listed and secure lid. Select "Batters". Allow batter to rest 5 minutes. Heat griddle or other pan over medium to medium high heat and grease. Pour approximately ¼ cup batter onto heated pan and cook approximately 1 minute or until bubbles break the surface of the pancake and the underside is golden brown. Flip and cook for approximately 30 seconds. Repeat with remaining batter. Serve immediately or keep warm in the oven at 200°F loosely wrapped in foil.

Whole Grain Pumpkin Pancakes

Servings 9
Serving Size 2 pancakes
Calories 210
Fat 4 g
Saturated Fat 1 g
Cholesterol 25 mg
Sodium 310 mg
Carbohydrates 35 g
Fiber 5 g
Sugar 10 g
Protein 9 g

Slightly sweet pancakes which are moist, fluffy and perfectly paired with toasted pecans and maple syrup. If you have extras, store them in the freezer and toast or warm them in the morning for breakfast.

WildSide Jar

1 C rolled oats
2 ¼ C milk
1 ¾ C whole white wheat flour
¾ C pumpkin purée
1 Tbsp canola oil
2 lg eggs
⅓ C brown sugar
1 tsp ground cinnamon
½ tsp ground nutmeg
¼ tsp ground ginger
2 tsp vanilla extract
½ tsp kosher salt
2 Tbsp nonfat dry milk
2 tsp baking powder
½ tsp baking soda

Add oats and milk to jar and secure lid. Select "Batters". Add remaining ingredients to jar and secure lid. Select "Batters" and rest batter for 5 minutes. Heat griddle or other pan over medium to medium-high heat and grease. Pour approximately ⅓ cup batter onto heated pan and cook approximately 1 minute or until bubbles break the surface of the pancake and the underside is golden brown. Flip and cook for approximately 30 seconds. Repeat with remaining batter. Serve immediately or keep warm in the oven at 200°F loosely wrapped in foil.

For banana pancakes, substitute pumpkin with ripe banana and add some walnuts for a little crunch.

Lemon Curd Pancakes

These light lemony pancakes are moist and perfectly paired with fresh raspberries and a lemon glaze.

Servings 7
Serving Size 2 pancakes
Calories 150
Fat 1.5 g
Saturated Fat 0.5 g
Cholesterol 35 mg
Sodium 380 mg
Carbohydrates 27 g
Fiber 0 g
Sugar 7 g
Protein 8 g

FourSide Jar

½ lemon
1 ½ C low-fat buttermilk
1 whole egg and 1 egg white
⅓ C low-fat cottage cheese
3 Tbsp brown sugar
1 ½ C all-purpose flour
1 tsp baking soda
½ tsp kosher salt

Use a paring knife to peel the lemon for zest. Add zest pieces with remaining ingredients to jar in order listed and secure lid. Select "Batters". Pour ¼ cup of batter per pancake onto heated and greased griddle or other pan. Cook about 1 minute or until bubbles break the surface of the pancake and the underside is golden brown. Flip and cook for about 30 seconds or until done. Repeat with remaining batter. Serve immediately or keep warm in the oven at 200°F loosely wrapped in foil.

Popovers

This American version of Yorkshire pudding can be served with marmalade and fresh fruit at breakfast or add some grated cheese and herbs for a more savory accompaniment to lunch or dinner. Remember to heat the pan before pouring the batter and once the popovers are in the oven - no peeking.

Servings 6
Serving Size 1 popover
Total Calories 200
Total Fat 9 g
Sat Fat 5 g
Cholesterol 125 mg
Sodium 260 mg
Carbohydrates 23 g
Fiber <1 g
Sugar 3 g
Protein 8 g

Either Jar

1 ¼ C milk
3 lg eggs
½ tsp kosher salt
1 Tbsp butter, melted
1 ¼ C all-purpose flour
2 Tbsp butter, cut into 6 even pieces

Preheat oven to 400°F and grease popover pan. Add ingredients to jar in order listed except the 2 tablespoons butter cut into 6 even pieces and secure lid. Select "Batters". Preheat popover pan in oven for 2 minutes. Remove preheated pan and place 1 small piece of butter in each cup and place pan back in oven until butter is melted. Again, remove the pan and fill each cup half full with batter. Bake for 20 minutes. Reduce temperature to 300°F and continue baking for 12-15 minutes.

Carrot Cake Hotcakes

Servings 7
Serving Size 2 pancakes
Calories 160
Fat 4 g
Saturated Fat 0 g
Cholesterol 30 mg
Sodium 230 mg
Carbohydrates 27 g
Fiber 3 g
Sugar 9 g
Protein 5 g

No scraped knuckles from hand grating for this hearty pancake that has a little crunch of walnut and a bite of bright carrot flavor.

WildSide Jar

1 ½ C baby carrots
¾ C low-fat buttermilk
1 lg egg
1 Tbsp canola oil
¼ C brown sugar
2 tsp baking powder
1 tsp ground cinnamon
¼ tsp kosher salt
⅛ tsp ground nutmeg
1 ½ tsp vanilla extract
⅔ C whole wheat flour
½ C all-purpose flour
¼ C walnuts

Add carrots to jar, fill with enough water to cover the carrots and secure lid. Press "Pulse" 10-12 times until carrot is chopped to desired size. Strain carrots, drain excess water and set aside. Add remaining ingredients to jar, except walnuts and chopped carrots, and secure lid. Select "Batters". Add walnuts to jar and secure lid. Press "Pulse" 6-8 times until nuts are chopped to desired size. Add chopped carrots to jar and secure lid. Press "Pulse" 1-2 times to incorporate grated carrots; do not over blend. Heat griddle or other pan over medium to medium high heat and grease. Scoop or pour approximately ⅓ cup batter onto heated griddle and cook approximately 1 minute or until bubbles break the surface of the pancake and the underside is golden brown. Flip and cook for approximately 30 seconds. Repeat with remaining batter. Serve immediately or keep warm in the oven at 200°F loosely wrapped in foil.

If you don't prefer the carrot crunch, microwave the grated carrots a couple minutes to soften them. Don't forget to drain excess water.

For 100% whole grain pancakes, use all whole wheat flour.

Puffed Apple Pancake

Servings 4
Serving Size 1 piece
Calories 370
Fat 16 g
Sat Fat 9 g
Cholesterol 190 mg
Sodium 400 mg
Carbohydrates 48 g
Fiber 2 g
Sugar 21 g
Protein 10 g

This breakfast or brunch treat has the texture of a classic baked pancake yet rises like Yorkshire pudding. Dust powdered sugar over the pancake after it's baked and serve with fresh berries.

Either Jar

4 Tbsp butter
4 Tbsp brown sugar, divided
½ tsp ground cinnamon
2 medium apples, peeled, cored and thinly sliced
¾ C milk
3 lg eggs
½ C all-purpose flour
½ tsp kosher salt
½ tsp vanilla extract

Preheat oven to 400°F. Heat a 10" or 12" ovenproof skillet or fry pan over medium heat, melt butter and stir in 1 tablespoon brown sugar and cinnamon. Add sliced apple and sauté, stirring occasionally, until apples begin to soften and brown, approximately 5 minutes. Spread sautéed apple slices evenly in pan and set aside.

In jar, add milk, eggs, remaining brown sugar, flour, salt and vanilla extract and secure lid. Select "Batters".

Pour batter over apples in pan. Bake pancake until puffed and brown, approximately 16-20 minutes. Dust with powder sugar and serve warm.

Crêpes

A simple recipe for breakfast or dinner with only four ingredients.

Either Jar

2 lg eggs
1 Tbsp butter, melted
1 ½ C milk
1 C all-purpose flour

Add ingredients to jar in order listed and secure lid. Press "Batters". Place the crêpe batter in the refrigerator for 1 hour prior to cooking crêpes. Heat a skillet or crêpe pan over medium heat and lightly coat with oil or cooking spray. For each crêpe, pour 1/4 cup batter into center of pan and swirl pan gently to distribute batter in a thin layer. Cook for 1 minute or until the top begins to dry out and underneath is lightly golden. Flip and cook an additional 30 seconds until done. Repeat with remaining batter. Stack completed crêpes on a plate with wax paper between each crêpe to prevent sticking. Fill with desired fillings or toppings.

For a sweet variation, follow directions above and add 2 tablespoons of sugar and 1 teaspoon vanilla extract to jar before blending.

For a savory variation, follow directions above and add ¼ teaspoon salt to jar before blending. After the "Batters" cycle is complete, add 2-4 tablespoons fresh herbs and secure lid. Press "Pulse" 4-6 times to incorporate and chop herbs.

Banana Blueberry Muffins

Servings 12
Serving Size 1 muffin
Calories 170
Fat 3.5 g
Saturated Fat 0.5 g
Cholesterol 35 mg
Sodium 160 mg
Carbohydrates 31 g
Fiber 3 g
Sugar 12 g
Protein 4 g

Prepare a different muffin variety every week of the year to keep breakfast boredom from setting in by using seasonal ingredients and multi-grain combinations.

WildSide Jar

2 ripe bananas
2 lg eggs
⅓ C low-fat plain yogurt
2 Tbsp canola oil
⅔ C brown sugar
1 tsp vanilla extract
1 ¼ C whole wheat flour
1 C all-purpose flour
2 tsp baking powder
½ tsp ground cinnamon
½ tsp salt
¾ C blueberries

Preheat oven to 350°F. Add bananas, eggs, yogurt, oil, brown sugar and vanilla to jar and secure lid. Select "Batters". Add remaining ingredients, except blueberries, and secure lid. Press "Pulse" 4–6 times or until dry ingredients are incorporated. Use a spatula to fold in blueberries. Pour batter into a greased muffin tin or a tin lined with paper cups. Bake 22–25 minutes until done.

Cranberry Bran Muffins

Servings 12
Serving Size 1 muffin
Calories 200
Fat 7 g
Saturated Fat 1 g
Cholesterol 35 mg
Sodium 45 mg
Carbohydrates 33 g
Fiber 4 g
Sugar 14 g
Protein 5 g

Make these muffins for morning breakfasts on the go. Store them in the freezer and grab one before you run out the door.

Either Jar

1 C milk
¼ C agave nectar
¼ C molasses
¼ C canola oil
2 eggs
1 C whole wheat pastry flour
1 C oat bran
½ C wheat germ
1 tsp baking powder
1 tsp ground cinnamon
1 ¼ C dried cranberries

Preheat oven to 375°F. Add milk, agave nectar, molasses, oil and eggs to jar and secure lid. Select "Batters". Add remaining ingredients to jar except dried cranberries and secure lid. Press "Pulse" 4–6 times or until dry ingredients are incorporated; do not over blend. Add dried cranberries to jar and incorporate with spoon or spatula. Allow batter to sit a few minutes. Pour batter into greased muffin tin or a tin lined with paper cups. Bake 20 minutes until done.

Apple Spice Muffins

Enjoy these fresh muffins made with warming spices and cooked apple bits.

Servings 12
Serving Size 1 muffin
Calories 160
Fat 3.5 g
Saturated Fat 2.5 g
Cholesterol 0 mg
Sodium 180 mg
Carbohydrates 30 g
Fiber 3 g
Sugar 14 g
Protein 4 g

FourSide Jar

1 C low-fat buttermilk
2 medium apples, quartered, cored and divided
¾ C sucanat
2 lg eggs
2 Tbsp coconut oil or butter
1 tsp vanilla extract
¾ tsp pumpkin pie spice
½ tsp kosher salt
1 Tbsp baking powder
2 C all-purpose or whole wheat flour, divided

Preheat oven to 375°F. Add buttermilk, half an apple, sucanat, eggs, coconut oil, vanilla extract, pumpkin pie spice and salt to jar and secure lid. Select "Batters". Add baking powder, 1 cup flour, remaining apple and last cup of flour and secure lid. Press "Pulse" 6-8 times or until dry ingredients are barely incorporated and apples are chopped in bits; do not over blend. Allow batter to sit 5 minutes. Pour batter into greased muffin tin. Bake 16–18 minutes until done.

For an extra special treat, sprinkle your favorite streusel atop the muffins before baking.

Bars and Cereals

Easy Homemade Granola

Servings 12
Serving Size ½ cup
Calories 300
Fat 13 g
Saturated Fat 2 g
Cholesterol 0 mg
Sodium 30 mg
Carbohydrates 43 g
Fiber 3 g
Sugar 20 g
Protein 6 g

Skip the supermarket stuff and make your own granola. Serve it at breakfast atop applesauce or yogurt, sprinkle on your baked sweet potato at dinner or pair with frozen yogurt at dessert.

FourSide Jar

3 C rolled oats
½ C sunflower seeds, hulled
½ C coconut, shredded, unsweetened
½ C flaxseeds
½ C walnuts
2 Tbsp canola oil
½ C honey
⅛ tsp kosher salt
½ tsp vanilla extract
½ C raisins
½ C dried cranberries

Preheat oven to 350°F. Spread oats*, sunflower seeds and coconut out on a parchment lined jelly roll pan. Toast in oven for 10 minutes, stirring once. Add flaxseeds to jar and secure lid. Press "Speed Up" to Speed 3 and allow full cycle to run. Set ground flaxseed aside in mixing bowl. Add walnuts to jar and secure lid. Press "Pulse" 3–5 times. Dump chopped walnuts into mixing bowl with flaxseed. Add oil, honey, salt and vanilla to jar and secure lid. Press "Pulse" 4–6 times until blended. Remove toasted mixture from oven and add ground flaxseed, walnuts, raisins and dried cranberries to toasted oats. Pour honey mixture over granola and stir all ingredients together. Return jelly roll pan to oven for 8–12 minutes. Remove from oven, cool and store in airtight container.

*For the gluten intolerant, ensure your oats are gluten-free.

Add your favorite dried fruit (apricots, cherries, currants, dates, etc), try different nuts and seeds for variety (pecans, hazelnuts, pumpkin, etc), and spice it up with cinnamon or nutmeg.

Cream of Buckwheat

Servings 5
Serving Size 1 cup
Calories 250
Fat 11 g
Saturated Fat 9 g
Cholesterol 0 mg
Sodium 10 mg
Carbohydrates 35 g
Fiber 3 g
Sugar 11 g
Protein 5 g

A gluten-free cream of buckwheat made with coconut milk and sweetened with turbinado sugar. Buckwheat boasts a glucose and cholesterol lowering effect.

FourSide Jar

1 C buckwheat groats
3 ¼ C water
1 C coconut milk
¼ C turbinado sugar or sweetener of choice
2 tsp vanilla extract

Add buckwheat groats to jar and secure lid. Press "Speed Up" to Speed 3, run cycle for 15 seconds and press "Pulse" to stop cycle. Add water, coconut milk, sugar and vanilla to medium saucepan and whisk in ground buckwheat. Bring to boil and continue whisking for a few minutes until hot cereal has thickened.

Five Grain Cereal

Servings 9
Serving Size ⅓ cup
Calories 210
Fat 1.5 g
Saturated Fat 0 g
Cholesterol 0 mg
Sodium 0 mg
Carbohydrates 44 g
Fiber 5 g
Sugar 0 g
Protein 6 g

This whole grain cereal, served hot, is a great way to start your day.

Either Jar

1 C oat groats
½ C millet
½ C barley
½ C brown rice
½ C cornmeal

Add all ingredients to jar in order listed and secure lid. Press "Speed Up" to Speed 4, run for 10–12 seconds and press "Pulse" to stop cycle. Transfer freshly cut grains to resealable container.

To prepare hot cereal, add 1 cup water per ⅓ cup serving of five grain cereal to saucepan and whisk together. Bring cereal to boil, reduce heat and simmer for 3–5 minutes until thickened.

Try different grain and seed variations, such as teff, amaranth, flax and sunflower seeds, for a different taste, texture and nutrient profile.

Muesli Bars

Servings 24
Serving Size 1 bar
Calories 210
Fat 6 g
Saturated Fat 0.5 g
Cholesterol 0 mg
Sodium 115 mg
Carbohydrates 36 g
Fiber 2 g
Sugar 22 g
Protein 5 g

All the ingredients are bound together by a mixture of nut butter and agave nectar. Add your favorite nuts and dried fruit into the mix. Wrap up individual bars, store them in the freezer and grab one for wholesome snack while running errands.

FourSide Jar
½ C dried apples
½ C pecans
2 ½ C rolled oats
½ C soy flour
⅓ C wheat germ
¼ C sesame seeds
½ C raisins
1 Tbsp canola oil
1 C agave nectar
½ C almond butter
2 tsp vanilla extract
½ tsp kosher salt

Preheat oven to 325°F. Add apples to jar and secure lid. Press "Pulse" 6–8 times until apples are chopped to desired size and dump into mixing bowl. Add pecans to jar and secure lid. Press "Pulse" 4–6 times until pecans are chopped and dump into mixing bowl. Add next five ingredients to mixing bowl. Add oil, agave nectar, almond butter, vanilla and salt to jar in order listed and secure lid. Press "Pulse" 5–7 times and pour into mixing bowl. Using a spatula, mix ingredients then gently press into 9"x 13" greased baking pan. Bake 25 minutes until edges begin to brown.

Eggs and Protein

Breakfast Sausage

Servings 6
Serving Size 2-2" patties
Calories 120
Fat 4 g
Saturated Fat 1.5 g
Cholesterol 40 mg
Sodium 360 mg
Carbohydrates 2 g
Fiber 0 g
Sugar 2 g
Protein 17 g

A leaner substitution for the typical fatty sausage that doesn't skimp on taste. Instead of using pork butt and shank, select a leaner cut of boneless meat of your choice, such as turkey, chicken breast or boneless pork chops.

WildSide Jar
1 lb lean pork, cubed and divided
1 Tbsp maple syrup
1 tsp kosher salt
½ tsp ground black pepper
¼ tsp ground sage
¼ tsp dried thyme
⅛ tsp ground nutmeg
⅛ tsp ground cayenne pepper
⅛ tsp crushed red pepper

Add half of meat, the seasonings and the remaining meat to jar and secure lid. Press "Pulse" 8–12 times until ground to desired consistency; do not over blend. Form patties and cook immediately or store ground sausage in an airtight container and freeze for up to 2 months.

For Hot Italian Sausage, follow directions above except substitute the following spices:

 1 tsp kosher salt
¾ tsp dried Italian seasoning
½ tsp ground black pepper
½ tsp fennel seeds
½ tsp crushed red pepper
¼ tsp garlic powder
¼ tsp paprika
¼ tsp ground cayenne pepper

Potatoes and Greens Frittata

Servings 6
Serving Size 1 slice
Calories 210
Fat 13 g
Saturated Fat 4.5 g
Cholesterol 225 mg
Sodium 290 mg
Carbohydrates 14 g
Fiber 2 g
Sugar 3 g
Protein 12 g

A savory egg dish with vibrant flavor.

FourSide Jar 🄌

2 Yukon Gold potatoes, sliced ⅛" to ¼" thick
2 Tbsp olive oil, divided
4 cloves garlic, minced and divided
1 tsp paprika
1 red onion, sliced ⅛" thick
¼ tsp ground cayenne pepper
3 C chard, roughly chopped
1 C fresh parsley leaves, roughly chopped
6 lg eggs
1 ¼ C low-fat milk
2 oz Neufchâtel cheese
1 Tbsp flour
½ tsp kosher salt
½ C mozzarella cheese

Preheat oven to 400°F. Toss potatoes with 1 ½ tablespoons oil, half of garlic and paprika in a bowl. Lay seasoned potato slices flat on a parchment lined baking sheet and bake for 15–20 minutes, until fork tender. While potatoes are baking, toss onions and cayenne pepper with remaining oil and garlic. Transfer seasoned onions to a sauté pan and sweat onions, approximately 5–7 minutes. Add chard and parsley to sauté pan and wilt greens. Add remaining ingredients to jar except mozzarella cheese and secure lid. Select "Batters". Remove potatoes from oven and decrease oven temperature to 350°F. Layer potatoes in circular 9" greased pan. Next, layer greens and onions over the potatoes and sprinkle with mozzarella cheese. Pour egg blend over cheese and bake for 25–30 minutes until done.

Baked French Toast

Servings 8
Serving Size 1 piece
Calories 280
Fat 10 g
Sat Fat 4.5 g
Cholesterol 225 mg
Sodium 130 mg
Carbohydrates 35 g
Fiber 3 g
Sugar 15 g
Protein 12 g

A scrumptious and sugar-coated breakfast treat which is prepared the night before and baked in the morning.

Either Jar

16 oz loaf whole wheat French bread
8 lg eggs
1 ¾ C milk
1 tsp vanilla extract
¼ tsp ground cinnamon
¼ tsp ground nutmeg
½ C brown sugar
3 Tbsp butter, melted
2 Tbsp maple syrup

Slice French bread into 1" slices and arrange bread slices in 9"x 13" pan, overlapping the slices. Add eggs, milk, vanilla extract, cinnamon and nutmeg to jar and secure lid. Select "Batters". Pour egg blend over bread slices, making sure bread slices are covered evenly with egg blend. Cover and refrigerate overnight.

The next morning preheat oven to 350°F. In a small bowl, combine brown sugar, butter and maple syrup. Spread evenly over soaked bread slices. Bake uncovered until knife inserted in center comes out clean, about 40-45 minutes. Let stand a few minutes before serving.

Jams and Syrups

Strawberry Syrup

With only 40 calories per serving, you can be generous with this syrup that provides 40% of your daily vitamin C. This is perfect for whole grain waffles or pancakes to get your morning started. If you have any leftovers use this syrup to sweeten your next smoothie.

Either Jar

2 C strawberries
1 tsp fresh lemon juice
3 Tbsp honey or other sweetener

Add ingredients to jar in order listed and secure lid. Select "Syrups" and serve.

Servings 7
Serving Size ¼ cup
Calories 40
Fat 0 g
Saturated Fat 0 g
Cholesterol 0 mg
Sodium 0 mg
Carbohydrates 11 g
Fiber 1 g
Sugar 9 g
Protein 0 g

Raspberry Maple Syrup

This slightly sweet syrup is a great way to have your sweet bite with only half the calories of traditional maple syrup and the added plus of antioxidants.

FourSide Jar

½ C maple syrup
1 ½ C raspberries

Add ingredients to jar and secure lid. Select "Syrups" and serve.

Servings 5
Serving Size ¼ cup
Calories 100
Fat 0 g
Saturated Fat 0 g
Cholesterol 0 mg
Sodium 0 mg
Carbohydrates 24 g
Fiber 3 g
Sugar 18 g
Protein 1 g

Strawberry Freezer Jam

Enjoy the great taste of summer year-round with this quick, no cook recipe delicious on toast or pancakes. Remember when you've opened a new jar, start thawing the next jar in the refrigerator; this jam moves quick!

WildSide Jar
2 lbs strawberries, hulled
2 C sugar
2 Tbsp fresh lemon juice
3 oz liquid pectin

Add half of strawberries and sugar to jar and secure lid. Select "Sauces". Let blend stand for 5 minutes. Add other half of strawberries and secure lid. Press "Pulse" 4–6 times to crush strawberries. Add lemon juice and pectin and secure lid. Press "Pulse" 1–2 times. Let jam stand 5 minutes. Pour into clean, plastic or glass freezer jars and twist on lids. Store jars in refrigerator for 24 hours until set. Refrigerate up to 3 weeks or freeze for up to 1 year. Yields 5 (8 oz) containers of jam.

Try different tender fruits for best results, such as: peaches, cherries, apricots and other berries.

Apple Butter

Servings 24
Serving Size 1 Tbsp
Calories 15
Fat 0 g
Saturated Fat 0 g
Cholesterol 0 mg
Sodium 0 mg
Carbohydrates 4 g
Fiber 0 g
Sugar 3 g
Protein 0 g

Dates and molasses are used to sweeten this scrumptious and tempting topping for crêpes, french toast or pancakes. Try a scoop of this in your morning bowl of steel cut oats with a little almond milk.

FourSide Jar

½ C warm water
1 tsp fresh lemon juice
2 Tbsp molasses
2 apples, peeled, sliced and steamed
3 soft dates, pitted
1"x 1" piece lemon zest
½ tsp ground cinnamon

Add ingredients to jar in order listed and secure lid. Select "Smoothie". Serve or store in refrigerator.

Dips

Classification Icon Key . . . . XXX-XXI

Dips

Easy Salsa

Serve this slightly chunky salsa with homemade baked tortilla chips. To move this mild salsa up on the Scoville scale, add a little cayenne pepper or fresh jalapeños.

Servings 9
Serving Size ¼ cup
Calories 15
Fat 1 g
Saturated Fat 0 g
Cholesterol 0 mg
Sodium 200 mg
Carbohydrates 3 g
Fiber < 1 g
Sugar 2 g
Protein 0 g

FourSide Jar 24

4 oz can green chiles, not drained
1 Tbsp fresh lime juice
1 clove garlic, quartered
½ tsp kosher salt
¼ tsp cumin
14.5 oz can diced tomatoes, not drained
1 chunk onion, approximately 2 Tbsp
¼ C fresh cilantro leaves

Add green chilies, lime juice, garlic, salt and cumin and secure lid. Press "Pulse" 3–5 times. Add tomatoes, onion and cilantro and secure lid. Press "Pulse" 3–5 times and serve.

For Spicy Chipotle Salsa, follow instructions above, replacing can of green chiles for 2 chipotle chiles in adobo sauce, add 2 teaspoons adobo sauce and 1 fresh jalapeño pepper that is quartered with seeds and veins removed.

To make baked corn tortilla chips, cut corn tortillas into eighths. Spray with cooking spray and sprinkle with salt, cumin and chili pepper, or desired seasoning. Bake at 350°F for 6 minutes. Use a spatula to flip chips and cook another 5–8 minutes until crisp and golden.

Savory Appetizer Cheesecake

Serving this savory cheesecake with crudités is a great way to enjoy fresh vegetables.

Servings 20
Serving Size 1 slice
Calories 140
Fat 12 g
Saturated Fat 6 g
Cholesterol 50 mg
Sodium 280 mg
Carbohydrates 4 g
Fiber 0 g
Sugar 2 g
Protein 7 g

WildSide Jar

1 tsp butter
1 slice whole wheat bread, toasted and quartered
1 whole egg and 3 egg whites
4 (8 oz) pkgs Neufchâtel cheese, quartered
6 oz jar artichoke hearts packed in water, drained
2 green onions, trimmed and roughly chopped
1 clove garlic, roughly chopped
1 C feta cheese
½ tsp dried oregano
½ tsp dried basil

Preheat oven to 325°F. Butter and quarter toast. Add toast to jar and secure lid. Press "Pulse" 4–6 times or until desired crumb size is reached. Press crumb mixture onto bottom of 9" springform pan. Add eggs and Neufchâtel cheese to jar and secure lid. Press "Pulse" 4–6 times. Add artichokes, green onions, garlic, feta cheese and herbs and secure lid. Press "Pulse" 3–5 times. Pour blend onto crust and bake 35 minutes until center is nearly set. Cool on rack for 30 min. Cover and chill at least 4 hours before serving.

Roasted Tomatillo and Cilantro Salsa

Servings 13
Serving Size ¼ cup
Calories 30
Fat 1.5 g
Saturated Fat 0 g
Cholesterol 0 mg
Sodium 300 mg
Carbohydrates 5 g
Fiber 1 g
Sugar 3 g
Protein < 1 g

This thick dip goes great with shrimp tacos or it can be used as a chip dip.

Either Jar
1 ½ lbs tomatillos, husked and rinsed
3 cloves garlic
1 medium onion, cut in eighths
4 jalapeño peppers, cored and seeded*
1 Tbsp olive oil
2 tsp kosher salt
1 C fresh cilantro leaves

Preheat oven to 375°F and toss first 6 ingredients in 9"x 13" glass baking dish. Roast until tomatillos and onions are soft, approximately 45 minutes. Allow contents of pan to cool. Transfer roasted ingredients to jar, add cilantro and secure lid. Press "Pulse" 8–10 times or until desired consistency is reached. Chill or serve at room temperature.

*To kick up the heat of this mild salsa, reserve some of the seeds and veins from the jalapeños to add before blending.

Note: To have roasted garlic on hand, cut off the top of a garlic bulb, drizzle with oil and wrap with foil. Bake in oven at the same time salsa ingredients are roasting.

For Enchilada Verde Sauce, use the WildSide jar and follow instructions as above. Before pressing "Pulse" to blend ingredients, add 2 cups chicken broth and ½ cup low-fat sour cream to the roasted salsa ingredients and secure lid. Select "Sauces".

Creamy Spinach Dip

For a savory snack that will help get more veggies into your day, take a dip and give this one a try.

FourSide Jar **2q**

2 tsp olive oil
1 clove garlic, roughly chopped
4 C spinach, lightly packed
½ tsp crushed red pepper
1 C low-fat cottage cheese
4 oz Neufchâtel cheese
¼ C Parmesan cheese

Servings 7
Serving Size ¼ cup
Calories 100
Fat 6 g
Saturated Fat 3 g
Cholesterol 15 mg
Sodium 260 mg
Carbohydrates 3 g
Fiber <1 g
Sugar 1 g
Protein 7 g

Heat oil in sauté pan and add garlic, spinach, and red pepper flakes. Cook until spinach is wilted and set aside. Add cottage cheese and Neufchâtel cheese to jar and secure lid. Select "Dips". Add Parmesan cheese and sautéed ingredients to jar and secure lid. Press "Pulse" 4–6 times until ingredients are incorporated; do not over blend. Serve or refrigerate until ready to use.

Creamy White Bean and Artichoke Dip

A great dip served cold or at room temperature with toasted pita slices, crackers or crudités.

FourSide Jar

⅓ C Vegan Mayo, see page 98
¾ C canned white beans
1 clove garlic
½ shallot, quartered
½ Tbsp apple cider vinegar
¼ tsp kosher salt
⅛ tsp ground mustard
⅛ tsp ground white pepper
14 oz can artichoke hearts, drained
4 oz can green chiles

Servings 10
Serving Size ¼ cup
Calories 80
Fat 5 g
Saturated Fat 0 g
Cholesterol 0 mg
Sodium 115 mg
Carbohydrates 8 g
Fiber 3 g
Sugar < 1 g
Protein 2 g

Add first 8 ingredients to jar in order listed and secure lid. Press "Speed Up" to Speed 1, run cycle for 15 seconds and press "Pulse" to stop cycle. Add artichoke hearts and green chiles to jar and secure lid. Press "Pulse" 5–7 times and serve.

Salmon Pâté

Servings 6
Serving Size ¼ cup
Calories 90
Fat 5 g
Saturated Fat 2.5 g
Cholesterol 25 mg
Sodium 250 mg
Carbohydrates 2 g
Fiber 0 g
Sugar 1 g
Protein 11 g

A delicious smooth spread great for crackers or a wonderful filling for tea sandwiches.

FourSide Jar 2x|

½ C fat-free Greek yogurt
4 oz Neufchâtel cheese
½ clove garlic, halved
8 oz salmon, steamed or canned; deboned
½ tsp dried dill
½ tsp prepared horseradish
¼ tsp kosher salt
⅛ tsp ground white pepper

Add yogurt, Neufchâtel cheese, garlic and salmon to jar and secure lid. Select "Sauces". Add remaining ingredients to jar in order listed and secure lid. Press "Pulse" 3–5 times until ingredients are evenly mixed. Serve immediately or refrigerate in desired mold.

Try adding a touch of all-natural liquid smoke to add depth of flavor.

Baba Ganoush

Servings 7
Serving Size ¼ cup
Calories 70
Fat 4.5 g
Saturated Fat 0.5 g
Cholesterol 0 mg
Sodium 60 mg
Carbohydrates 7 g
Fiber 3 g
Sugar 2 g
Protein 2 g

For a great entertaining idea serve this delicious and nutritious dip with veggies and pita bread. Garnish this Middle-Eastern dip with paprika, olive oil and chopped parsley.

FourSide Jar 2x|

1 large eggplant, halved
¼ C Tahini, see page 97
3 cloves garlic, halved
¼ C fresh lemon juice
½ tsp cumin
¼ tsp sea salt
1 Tbsp olive oil, optional garnish
½ tsp paprika, optional garnish
2 Tbsp chopped parsley, optional garnish

Preheat oven to 400°F. Prick eggplant with fork several times and place flesh-side down on a parchment lined baking sheet. Bake for 30 minutes. Cool slightly and peel off eggplant skin. Add cooked eggplant flesh and remaining ingredients, except optional garnishes, to jar and secure lid. Select "Dips". Garnish and serve.

Hummus

Hummus is an inexpensive, high-fiber and protein-packed food; yet only a few households dabble with this dip. This Middle Eastern mixture of chickpeas, also known as garbanzo beans, and tahini has endless possibilities so there's no hummus humdrum.

Servings 7
Serving Size ¼ cup
Calories 100
Fat 7 g
Saturated Fat 1 g
Cholesterol 0 mg
Sodium 350 mg
Carbohydrates 12 g
Fiber 3 g
Sugar 1 g
Protein 5 g

FourSide Jar 🔵

2 Tbsp olive oil
2 Tbsp fresh lemon juice
2 Tbsp Tahini, see page 97
1 clove garlic, quartered
½ tsp kosher salt
15 oz can chickpeas, drained and ¼ C liquid reserved

Add ingredients, including the ¼ cup reserved garbanzo bean liquid, to jar in order listed and secure lid. Select "Sauces" and serve.

For the following hummus variations, follow the instructions above except add these additional ingredients or make changes as noted.

Smoky Sun-dried Tomato Hummus:
4 slices sun-dried tomatoes, packed in oil
¼ tsp smoked paprika
Increase reserved liquid to ⅓ cup
Repeat the "Sauces" cycle to ensure sun-dried tomatoes blend smoothly.

Kalamata Olive Hummus:
½ C Kalamata olives, pitted
Reduce salt to ¼ tsp kosher salt
Increase reserved liquid to ⅓ cup

Roasted Garlic Hummus:
1 roasted garlic bulb, cloves squeezed out of skin
Increase reserved liquid to ⅓ cup

Chipotle Hummus:
1 chipotle pepper in adobo sauce
1 tsp adobo sauce

Lime Cilantro Hummus:
Replace lemon juice with lime juice
1" x 1" piece lime zest
1 C cilantro leaves, loosely packed
Increase reserved liquid to ⅓ cup

Black Bean Hummus:
Replace chickpeas with black beans and reserve black bean liquid
½ tsp ground cumin
¼ tsp ground cayenne pepper
¼ tsp smoked paprika

Spicy Shrimp Dip

Servings 7
Serving Size ¼ cup
Calories 80
Fat 4 g
Saturated Fat 2 g
Cholesterol 45 mg
Sodium 160 mg
Carbohydrates 2 g
Fiber 0 g
Sugar 1 g
Protein 7 g

Serve this dip in individual tomato cups as perfectly portioned appetizers accompanied by crostini.

FourSide Jar 🔵

½ C fat-free Greek yogurt
4 oz Neufchâtel cheese
2 chunks onion, approximately ¼ cup
1 jalapeño pepper, cored and seeded*
1 tsp fresh lemon juice
½ tsp kosher salt
½ tsp garlic powder
½ tsp paprika
¼ tsp ground black pepper
½ lb shrimp, peeled, deveined and steamed

Add all ingredients except shrimp to jar and secure lid. Press "Pulse" 4–6 times in order to chop jalapeño and onion. Add shrimp to jar and secure lid. Press "Pulse" 3–5 times until desired consistency is reached.

*To kick up the heat of this dip, reserve some of the seeds and veins from the jalapeños to add before blending.

For tomato cups, slice off ½" from top of each vine-ripened tomato. With small spoon, gently scoop out and discard pulp to create hollow shell. Turn tomatoes upside down on large plate lined with paper towel to drain tomatoes while preparing the dip. Once drained, fill tomato cups with dip.

Basic Guacamole

Servings 7
Serving Size ¼ cup
Calories 100
Fat 9 g
Saturated Fat 1 g
Cholesterol 0 mg
Sodium 115 mg
Carbohydrates 6 g
Fiber 4 g
Sugar 0 g
Protein 1 g

Instead of using a molcajete, toss your guacamole ingredients in the blender and whip up this dip filled with monounsaturated fats, oleic and linoleic acids, which may help lower or control cholesterol levels.

FourSide Jar

3 Tbsp fresh lime juice
1 small shallot, halved
1 clove garlic, quartered
½ tsp kosher salt
3 ripe avocados, peeled and pitted
⅓ C fresh cilantro leaves

Add first 4 ingredients to jar in order listed and secure lid. Press "Pulse" 2–3 times. Add remaining ingredients and secure lid. Press "Pulse" 8–10 times and serve.

Chocolate Honey Nut Fondue

Servings 16
Serving Size 3 Tbsp
Calories 250
Fat 18 g
Saturated Fat 7 g
Cholesterol 5 mg
Sodium 85 mg
Carbohydrates 18 g
Fiber 3 g
Sugar 12 g
Protein 6 g

Get your favorite fruit ready to dip into this indulgent treat. This is an easy dessert to whip up quickly for a group of friends.

Either Jar

1 C half and half, warmed
12 oz semi-sweet chocolate chips
3 Tbsp honey
1 C chunky peanut butter

Add half and half, chocolate, and honey to jar and secure lid. Select "Fondues". Add peanut butter and secure lid. Press "Pulse" 4–6 times or until blended to desired consistency. Pour into fondue pot to keep warm.

Dressings

Dressings

Raspberry Vinaigrette

This dressing is delicious served on a bed of greens sprinkled with fresh raspberries and caramelized walnuts.

Servings 10
Serving Size 2 Tbsp
Calories 70
Fat 6 g
Saturated Fat 0 g
Cholesterol 0 mg
Sodium 100 mg
Carbohydrates 6 g
Fiber 0 g
Sugar 4 g
Protein 0 g

FourSide Jar
½ C water
¼ C olive oil
¼ C red wine vinegar
2 Tbsp honey
½ tsp ground mustard
½ tsp kosher salt
1 C raspberries

Add ingredients to jar in order listed and secure lid. Select "Dressings" and serve.

Strawberry Ginger Dressing

Only four ingredients in this simple dressing helps build a better salad.

Servings 12
Serving Size 2 Tbsp
Calories 20
Fat 0 g
Saturated Fat 0 g
Cholesterol 0 mg
Sodium 0 mg
Carbohydrates 5 g
Fiber 1 g
Sugar 4 g
Protein 0 g

FourSide Jar
2 C strawberries, hulled
3 Tbsp fresh lime juice
2 Tbsp honey
1 chunk ginger root, peeled, approximately 1 Tbsp

Add ingredients to jar in order listed and secure lid. Select "Dressings" and serve.

Ginger Dressing

Serve with a crisp salad of romaine lettuce, cucumbers and carrots, or try on cold noodles for an Asian noodle dish.

Servings 10
Serving Size 2 Tbsp
Calories 90
Fat 8 g
Saturated Fat 1 g
Cholesterol 0 mg
Sodium 140 mg
Carbohydrates 4 g
Fiber 0 g
Sugar 3 g
Protein 0 g

FourSide Jar

⅓ C orange juice
3 Tbsp sesame oil
3 Tbsp vegetable oil
2 Tbsp balsamic vinegar
2 Tbsp water
2 Tbsp soy sauce
1 Tbsp honey
2 chunks ginger root, peeled, approximately 2½ Tbsp
1 Tbsp Dijon mustard
2 green onions, trimmed and quartered
1 clove garlic, quartered

Add ingredients to jar in order listed and secure lid. Select "Dressings" and serve.

Garlic Blue Cheese Dressing

A low-fat blue cheese dressing great on a bibb lettuce salad or on a roast beef sandwich.

Servings 16
Serving Size 2 Tbsp
Calories 20
Fat 0.5 g
Saturated Fat 0 g
Cholesterol < 5 mg
Sodium 85 mg
Carbohydrates < 1 g
Fiber 0 g
Sugar < 1 g
Protein 2 g

FourSide Jar

¼ C low-fat buttermilk
1 C low-fat cottage cheese
1 clove garlic
2 oz blue cheese

Add first 3 ingredients to jar and secure lid. Select "Dressings". Add blue cheese and secure lid. Press "Pulse" 3–4 times. Serve or refrigerate for up to 3 days.

Sans the blue cheese, this dressing is a great base for low-fat homemade ranch. Add the above ingredients to jar except the blue cheese; then add a ¼ teaspoon each of onion powder, salt, and black pepper and secure lid. Press "Batters". Add ¼ teaspoon dill, ½ teaspoon dried parsley, and ½ teaspoon dried chives to jar and secure lid. Press "Pulse" 3-4 times and serve.

Bloody Mary Dressing

Servings 14
Serving Size 2 Tbsp
Calories 45
Fat 4 g
Saturated Fat 1 g
Cholesterol 0 mg
Sodium 42 mg
Carbohydrates 2 g
Fiber 0 g
Sugar 1 g
Protein 0 g

This salad dressing, served in a shot glass, is perfectly portioned. Serve this dressing over leafy greens with avocado slices and steamed shrimp.

Either Jar
¼ C pickle juice
⅔ C low-sodium tomato juice
¼ C olive oil
2 Tbsp fresh lemon juice
2 Tbsp tomato paste
1 clove garlic
¼ tsp ground black pepper
1 Tbsp prepared horseradish
1 Tbsp Worcestershire sauce
¼ tsp celery seed
¼ tsp dried dill
1 oz citrus vodka, optional

Add ingredients to jar in order listed and secure lid. Select "Dressings" and serve.

Roasted Red Pepper Dressing

Servings 10
Serving Size 2 Tbsp
Calories 70
Fat 7 g
Saturated Fat 1 g
Cholesterol 0 mg
Sodium 100 mg
Carbohydrates 2 g
Fiber < 1 g
Sugar 1 g
Protein 0 g

Dress a salad of mixed greens with grape tomatoes, sliced red onion, cucumber, feta, and chickpeas; then top the cool crunch of fresh veggies with the tang of this vinaigrette.

FourSide Jar
⅓ C olive oil
¼ C water
3 Tbsp white distilled vinegar
2 roasted red peppers
1 clove garlic
½ tsp kosher salt
⅛ tsp smoked paprika
⅛ tsp cayenne pepper

Add ingredients to jar in order listed and secure lid. Select "Dressings" and serve.

To roast red peppers, preheat oven to high broil. On a baking sheet, add the red peppers and broil for 4-6 minutes until blackened. Rotate red peppers and broil again, repeating this step until all sides are roasted. Remove red peppers from oven and place in a covered container for 15 minutes to allow steam to loosen the skin from red peppers. Gently peel red peppers and discard skin. Core and seed the red peppers before use.

Creamy Miso Dressing

Servings 7
Serving Size 2 Tbsp
Calories 80
Fat 8 g
Saturated Fat 1 g
Cholesterol 0 mg
Sodium 150 mg
Carbohydrates 3 g
Fiber < 1 g
Sugar < 1 g
Protein < 1 g

This dairy-free dressing is light with a hint of miso and sesame. Serve this with a salad dressed up with bean sprouts, water chestnuts, peanuts or other Asian flavors.

FourSide Jar
¼ C water
3 Tbsp fresh lemon juice
2 Tbsp sesame oil
2 Tbsp olive oil
2 Tbsp brown rice miso
1 chunk onion, approximately 2 Tbsp
1 clove garlic, quartered

Add ingredients to jar in order listed and secure lid. Select "Dressings" and serve.

Ruby Poppy Dressing

This deliciously light and tangy dressing is great on top of a bed of spinach with sliced strawberries, grapefruit sections and roasted pecans.

Servings 10
Serving Size 2 Tbsp
Calories 30
Fat 2 g
Saturated Fat 0 g
Cholesterol 0 mg
Sodium 1 mg
Carbohydrates 4 g
Fiber 0 g
Sugar 3 g
Protein 0 g

FourSide Jar **2x**
¾ C red grapefruit juice
1 Tbsp olive oil
1 Tbsp honey
2 (1"x 1") pieces orange zest
2 (1"x 1") pieces grapefruit zest
2 strawberries, hulled
½ tsp ground mustard
⅛ tsp xanthan gum
2 tsp poppy seeds

Add ingredients to jar in order listed, except xanthan gum and poppy seeds, and secure lid. Select "Dressings". Remove vented gripper lid insert and add xanthan gum. Press "Pulse" 3–5 times or until the dressing becomes slightly more viscous. Add the poppy seeds and press "Pulse" 2-3 times and serve.

Note: Xanthan gum is found near gluten–free baking items at your local grocers or health food store.

Caesar Dressing

A creamy Caesar dressing that is thick enough to use as a dip. Best when allowed to sit refrigerated overnight and marry the flavors before tossing with romaine lettuce, homemade croutons and thin slices of Parmesan cheese.

Servings 14
Serving Size 2 Tbsp
Calories 150
Fat 16 g
Sat Fat 2.5 g
Cholesterol 15 mg
Sodium 180 mg
Carbohydrates 0 g
Fiber 0 g
Sugar 0 g
Protein 1 g

FourSide Jar
1 C olive oil
¼ C water
2 Tbsp lemon juice
1 Tbsp white wine vinegar
1 tsp kosher salt
1 tsp Worcestershire sauce
1 tsp Dijon mustard
¼ tsp ground black pepper
1 lg egg yolk*
2 cloves garlic
¼ C grated Parmesan cheese

Add ingredients to jar in order listed and secure lid. Select "Dressings" and serve.

*Consuming raw or undercooked egg(s) or egg products can increase your risk of food born illness. To reduce the risk, use pasteurized eggs.

Parsley Tofu Dressing

A healthy way to enjoy a ranch-like dressing for a salad or dip.

FourSide Jar

4 oz soft tofu
1 Tbsp apple cider vinegar
1 Tbsp fresh lemon juice
1 Tbsp vegetable oil
¼ tsp kosher salt
¼ tsp black pepper
½ clove garlic
1 Tbsp dried parsley

Add ingredients to jar and secure lid. Select "Dressings" and serve.

Sauces, Spreads and Marinades

Sauces

Hollandaise Sauce

Instead of whisking away in the kitchen, try this simple recipe for a light, lemony butter emulsion in the blender.

FourSide Jar

3 egg yolks*
1 Tbsp fresh lemon juice
½ tsp kosher salt
⅛ tsp ground cayenne pepper
9 Tbsp unsalted butter, melted

Add first 4 ingredients to jar and secure lid. Select "Sauces". Remove vented gripper lid insert, press "Speed Up" to Speed 1 and slowly drizzle melted butter through vent over duration of cycle. Keep sauce warm until serving.

*Consuming raw or undercooked egg(s) or egg products can increase your risk of food born illness. To reduce the risk, use pasteurized eggs.

Oven Roasted Tomato Sauce

A simple sauce to make, it will fill your home with a mouthwatering aroma.

FourSide Jar

2 lbs tomatoes, quartered
1 medium onion, roughly chopped
8 cloves garlic
3 Tbsp olive oil
2 Tbsp fresh oregano
1 tsp kosher salt

Preheat oven to 375°F and toss all ingredients in 9"x 13" glass baking dish. Roast for 1 hour. Remove pan from oven, cool slightly and transfer all ingredients to jar and secure lid. Select "Sauces". Serve or store and refrigerate.

Thai Peanut Sauce

Servings 8
Serving Size 2 Tbsp
Calories 90
Fat 7 g
Saturated Fat 2 g
Cholesterol 0 mg
Sodium 190 mg
Carbohydrates 6 g
Fiber 1 g
Sugar 4 g
Protein 3 g

A highly flavored and multi-purpose sauce great for dipping, tossed with noodles for a cool salad, drizzled over sautéed vegetables or accompanied with shish kabobs.

FourSide Jar

¼ C coconut milk
2 Tbsp fresh lime juice
1 Tbsp soy sauce
1 Tbsp honey
1 clove garlic
1 Tbsp ginger root, peeled
1 tsp hot pepper sauce
⅓ C peanut butter

Add ingredients to jar in order listed and secure lid. Select "Sauces" and serve.

Roasty Red Enchilada Sauce

Servings 8
Serving Size ½ cup
Calories 60
Fat 4 g
Saturated Fat 0 g
Cholesterol 0 mg
Sodium 500 mg
Carbohydrates 5 g
Fiber 2 g
Sugar 3 g
Protein 2 g

This slightly smoky and savory sauce is gluten-free. Guajillo chiles are typically available in Latin food markets and some well-stocked grocery stores. If you have any leftovers, store in freezer in an airtight container.

Either Jar

3 dried guajillo chiles
15 oz can tomato sauce
1 ½ C vegetable broth
1 clove garlic
1 ½ Tbsp chili powder
2 Tbsp vegetable oil
1 ½ tsp paprika
½ tsp kosher salt
¼ tsp dried oregano
¼ tsp ground cumin

Toast guajillo chiles in a 400°F preheated oven or in a cast iron skillet over medium-high heat for 2–3 minutes until aromatic. Soak guajillos in hot water, up to 1 hour, and remove stems and seeds. Add chiles to jar with remaining ingredients in order listed and secure lid. Select "Soups". Pour into saucepan and simmer sauce until heated thoroughly. Serve atop your favorite enchiladas, approximately ½ cup per two enchiladas.

Basil Pistachio Pesto

Spread this flavorful pesto on crusty bread as an appetizer or toss with your favorite pasta to serve as an entrée or side dish.

FourSide Jar
½ C olive oil
2 cloves garlic, roughly chopped
3 C basil leaves, lightly packed
⅓ C shelled and roasted pistachios
½ C grated Parmesan cheese
¼ tsp kosher salt
¼ tsp ground black pepper

Add oil, garlic and basil to jar and push basil down into oil and secure lid. Press "Pulse" 6–8 times until basil is roughly chopped. Add the remaining ingredients in order listed and secure lid. Press "Pulse" 4–6 times until course purée texture is reached. Pesto will keep covered in refrigerator up to 3 days.

To reduce calories, substitute some of the olive oil with vegetable or chicken broth.

Curried Apricot Sauce

Servings 10
Serving Size 2 Tbsp
Calories 40
Fat 2.5 g
Saturated Fat 0 g
Cholesterol 0 mg
Sodium 15 mg
Carbohydrates 5 g
Fiber < 1 g
Sugar 8 g
Protein 0 g

A simple sauce with sharp flavor that is great for dipping shrimp or grilled shish kabobs.

FourSide Jar
15 oz can apricots, drained
2 Tbsp mayonnaise
1 Tbsp honey
1 tsp curry powder

Add ingredients to jar in order listed and secure lid. Select "Sauces" and serve.

For a tangy and lower-calorie version, substitute plain yogurt for the mayonnaise.

Cilantro Chili Sauce

A quick and delicious sauce great for dipping spring rolls.

FourSide Jar
¼ C water
½ C sweet chili sauce
2 tsp ginger root, peeled
2 tsp tamarind paste
1 C fresh cilantro leaves

Add first 4 ingredients to jar in order listed and secure lid. Press "Pulse" 4–6 times. Add cilantro leaves to jar until touching the wet ingredients and secure lid. Press "Pulse" 3–5 times until cilantro leaves are roughly chopped.

Servings 8
Serving Size 2 Tbsp
Calories 30
Fat 0 g
Saturated Fat 0 g
Cholesterol 0 mg
Sodium 140 mg
Carbohydrates 6 g
Fiber 0 g
Sugar 6 g
Protein 0 g

Spreads

Garden Cashew Cream

Vary the thickness of this soft and creamy cheese by using more or less water. It is a very versatile recipe that can be spread on crackers or used as a filling in a collard wrap.

FourSide Jar

2 Tbsp water
2 Tbsp fresh lemon juice
1 Tbsp Nama Shoyu
¼ C red bell pepper
2 Tbsp red onion
2 Tbsp nutritional yeast
1 clove garlic
1 C cashews, soaked for 2-4 hours and rinsed

Add ingredients to jar in order listed and secure lid. Select "Ice Cream" and serve.

Servings 8
Serving Size 2 Tbsp
Calories 80
Fat 6 g
Saturated Fat 1 g
Cholesterol 0 mg
Sodium 75 mg
Carbohydrates 5 g
Fiber < 1 g
Sugar 1 g
Protein 3 g

Garlic Basil Cheese Spread

A versatile recipe to be spread on pizza dough in place of pizza sauce, to stuff manicotti or to use in baked ziti with a white sauce.

FourSide Jar

¼ C milk
2 cloves garlic, quartered
½ C basil leaves, lightly packed
¾ C part-skim ricotta cheese
⅓ C shredded Parmesan cheese
¼ tsp kosher salt
⅛ tsp ground black pepper

Add ingredients to jar in order listed and secure lid. Select "Sauces". Use immediately or store in refrigerator for 1–2 days.

Servings 8
Serving Size 2 Tbsp
Calories 50
Fat 3 g
Saturated Fat 2 g
Cholesterol 10 mg
Sodium 140 mg
Carbohydrates 2 g
Fiber 0 g
Sugar 0 g
Protein 4 g

Almond Butter

For a twist on a classic, enjoy almond butter with celery and dried cranberries for "fire ants on a log."

FourSide Jar

3 C roasted and unsalted almonds
1 tsp kosher salt
2 Tbsp peanut or walnut oil

Add almonds and salt to jar and secure lid. Press "Speed Up" to Speed 1 and at 15 seconds press "Speed Up" to Speed 9 for remainder of cycle. Using a spatula, move contents of jar towards center of jar, add oil and secure lid. Press "Speed Up" to Speed 5 and run full cycle.

Peanut Butter

This homemade peanut butter is simply enticing and unadulterated. It takes a few cycles to transform whole peanuts to warm and creamy peanut butter.

FourSide Jar

3 C roasted and unsalted peanuts
1 tsp kosher salt
2 Tbsp peanut oil

Add peanuts and salt to jar and secure lid. Press "Speed Up" to Speed 1 and at 15 seconds press "Speed Up" to Speed 9 for remainder of cycle. Using a spatula, move peanuts towards center of jar, add oil and secure lid. Press "Speed Up" button to Speed 3 and run full cycle. Stir and secure lid. Press "Speed Up" to Speed 5 and run full cycle.

For peanut butter with no oil added, you need to blend the peanut butter for an additional cycle to ensure creamy and smooth peanut butter. After the second cycle, where the oil would be added, run an additional cycle at Speed 2 for a full cycle.

Butter

Servings 16
Serving Size 1 Tbsp
Calories 100
Fat 11 g
Saturated Fat 1 g
Cholesterol 40 mg
Sodium 10 mg
Carbohydrates 0 g
Fiber 0 g
Sugar 0 g
Protein 0 g

Whether you want a little honey butter on popovers or would like tarragon butter for steak, this recipe allows for versatility.

FourSide Jar
2 C whipping cream

Allow whipping cream to sit out for 30-45 minutes*. Add whipping cream to jar and secure lid. Press "Speed Up" to Speed 2, run cycle for 15–20 seconds and press "Pulse" to stop cycle. Using a spatula, move whipped cream towards center of jar and secure lid. Press "Pulse" and hold down, 2–3 seconds, until whipped cream has stopped blending. Using a spatula, move contents towards center of jar. Repeat this step of pulsing, stirring and securing lid 10–12 times. Once buttermilk begins to separate from butter curds, press "Pulse" for 2-3 seconds until solid butter curds separate from butter milk.

*Using cold cream to make butter will take more time to churn and transform to butter.

For Cilantro Lime Butter, add ¼ cup fresh cilantro leaves, 2 teaspoon lime zest and ½ teaspoon sea salt towards the end of pulsing and stirring step.

For Honey Butter, add ⅓ cup honey and stir or pulse into butter.

Mango Mustard

Servings 8
Serving Size 2 Tbsp
Calories 20
Fat 0 g
Saturated Fat 0 g
Cholesterol 0 mg
Sodium 70 mg
Carbohydrates 5 g
Fiber 0 g
Sugar 5 g
Protein 0 g

This sauce will add a tangy touch to any meal. Serve with grilled salmon or try over jerk chicken and rice.

FourSide Jar
1 ½ Tbsp apple cider vinegar
1 ½ Tbsp Dijon mustard
1 tsp honey
1 ripe mango, peeled and pitted

Add ingredients to jar and secure lid. Select "Sauces" and serve.

Blender Mayonnaise

Servings 16
Serving Size 1 Tbsp
Calories 120
Fat 13 g
Saturated Fat 1 g
Cholesterol 25 mg
Sodium 70 mg
Carbohydrates 0 g
Fiber 0 g
Sugar 0 g
Protein 0 g

Pure and preservative free mayonnaise that tastes great. Store it in the refrigerator and use it up within a few days.

FourSide Jar

2 egg yolks*
1 Tbsp white wine vinegar
½ tsp Dijon mustard
½ tsp kosher salt
⅞ C vegetable or canola oil, divided

Add yolks, vinegar, mustard, kosher salt and 3 tablespoon of oil to jar and secure lid. Press "Speed Up" to Speed 2 and allow full cycle to run. Again press "Speed Up" to Speed 2 and near the opening of the lid insert add ½ the oil in a slow steady stream over duration of the cycle. Repeat this step with the remaining oil. Use immediately or refrigerate for up to 1 week.

Note: During the final seconds of the last cycle if it appears the mayonnaise is nice and thick, press the "Pulse" button to stop the cycle, as the emulsification process has met its threshold.

*Consuming raw or undercooked egg(s) or egg products can increase your risk of food born illness. To reduce the risk, use pasteurized eggs.

For Aioli, follow directions above and add 2 quartered cloves garlic, when adding ingredients to first cycle and substitute half of canola or vegetable oil with olive oil.

For Spicy Sushi Mayo, follow directions above and substitute rice vinegar for white wine vinegar. In place of all vegetable or canola oil, use ½ cup chili oil, 6 tablespoons vegetable or canola oil and 2 tablespoons sesame oil.

Tahini

Similar to the texture of nut butter, tahini takes a little time to evolve from whole seeds to ground seeds to a crumbly paste and then finally to a smooth tahini.

WildSide Jar
¼ C olive oil
3 C hulled and toasted sesame seeds*

Servings 15
Serving Size 2 Tbsp
Calories 180
Fat 16 g
Saturated Fat 2 g
Cholesterol 0 mg
Sodium 10 mg
Carbohydrates 5 g
Fiber 2 g
Sugar 0 g
Protein 4 g

Add oil and seeds to jar and secure lid. Press "Speed Up" to Speed 2 and run full cycle. Using a spatula, move contents towards center of jar and secure lid. Press "Speed Up" to Speed 5 and run full cycle. Store in an airtight container in the refrigerator for 4-6 weeks.

*To toast hulled sesame seeds, preheat oven to 350°F. Spread sesame seeds on a jelly roll pan. Toast seeds for 10-12 minutes. To ensure even toasting, stir the sesame seeds after 5-6 minutes in oven, then finish toasting.

Chocolate Hazelnut Spread

A delicious, dairy-free spread that hits the spot for any chocolate lover. Serve with fresh fruit, use as a crêpe filling, spread onto your favorite bread, or enjoy it by the spoonful.

FourSide Jar
2 C hazelnuts
¼ C coconut oil, melted
¼ C cocoa powder
1 tsp vanilla extract
1 C powdered sugar

Servings 16
Serving Size 2 Tbsp
Calories 190
Fat 13 g
Saturated Fat 4 g
Cholesterol 0 mg
Sodium 0 mg
Carbohydrates 12 g
Fiber 2 g
Sugar 10 g
Protein 2 g

To toast hazelnuts, preheat oven to 350°F. Spread hazelnuts on shallow baking sheet and toast in oven until skins darken, approximately 8-10 minutes. To ensure even toasting, stir the hazelnuts after 4-5 minutes in oven, then finish toasting. Wrap the cooled hazelnuts in a clean kitchen towel and rub towel back and forth to remove most of the hazelnut skins. Add coconut oil and hazelnuts to jar and secure lid. Press "Speed Up" to Speed 1, run for 15 seconds and increase to Speed 9 for remainder of cycle . Stir hazelnut meal towards center of jar and secure lid. Press "Speed Up" to Speed 5 and run full cycle. Stir, secure lid and repeat this cycle two times. Add cocoa powder, vanilla extract and powdered sugar to jar and secure lid. Press "Speed Up" to Speed 5 and run full cycle. Store in an airtight container in the refrigerator for 4-6 weeks. Bring to room temperature before serving.

Vegan Mayo

Much less expensive than the store bought stuff, this thick and creamy mayo is delicious in a Waldorf salad with crisp apples and walnuts.

Servings 24
Serving Size 1 Tbsp
Calories 80
Fat 9 g
Saturated Fat 0.5 g
Cholesterol 0 mg
Sodium 35 mg
Carbohydrates 0 g
Fiber 0 g
Sugar 0 g
Protein 0 g

FourSide Jar

½ C unsweetened soy milk
2 tsp apple cider vinegar
½ tsp kosher salt
½ tsp agave nectar
¼ tsp ground mustard
1 C vegetable or canola oil

Add ingredients to jar, except oil, in order listed and secure lid. Press "Speed Up" to Speed 2 and near the opening of the lid insert add ½ the oil in a slow and steady stream over duration of the cycle. Press "Speed Up" to Speed 3 and add remaining oil in a slow and steady stream through opening near lid insert over duration of the cycle. Use immediately or refrigerate for up to 1 week.

Avocado Aioli

Use as a dip with crudités, sweep over your favorite bread for a sandwich spread or use to accompany grilled chicken or salmon.

Servings 8
Serving Size 2 Tbsp
Calories 40
Fat 3 g
Saturated Fat 0 g
Cholesterol 0 mg
Sodium 55 mg
Carbohydrates 2 g
Fiber 1 g
Sugar 0 g
Protein 1 g

FourSide Jar

½ C Greek yogurt
1 large ripe avocado, peeled and pitted
1 Tbsp fresh lime juice
1 clove garlic, quartered
¼ tsp kosher salt
⅛ tsp ground black pepper

Add ingredients to jar in order listed and secure lid. Select "Sauces".

For Avocado Wasabi Sauce, follow directions above and add ½ teaspoon wasabi powder to jar before blending.

Marinades

Beef Marinade

Use this savory marinade for any cut of beef. Marinate the meat for at least 1 hour or longer for more intense flavor.

FourSide Jar

⅓ C olive oil
¼ C fresh lemon juice
¼ C soy sauce
3 Tbsp Worcestershire sauce
1 clove garlic
1 Tbsp dried basil
½ Tbsp dried parsley
¼ tsp ground black pepper

Add all ingredients to jar in order as listed and secure lid. Select "Sauces".

Servings 8
Serving Size 2 Tbsp
Calories 90
Fat 9 g
Saturated Fat 1 g
Cholesterol 0 mg
Sodium 580 mg
Carbohydrates 3 g
Dietary Fiber 0 g
Sugars 1 g
Protein < 1 g

Lime Cilantro Marinade

Use as a marinade for fajitas or as a sauce drizzled over fish tacos with sliced cabbage and pico de gallo.

FourSide Jar

2 cloves garlic
2 chunks red onion, approximately ¼ C
4 limes, peeled and halved
⅓ C vegetable oil
1 Tbsp honey
½ C fresh cilantro leaves
½ tsp kosher salt
¼ tsp ground black pepper
¼ tsp dried oregano

Add ingredients to jar in order listed and secure lid. Select "Sauces".

Servings 10
Serving Size 2 Tbsp
Calories 80
Fat 7 g
Saturated Fat 0 g
Cholesterol 0 mg
Sodium 95 mg
Carbohydrates 5 g
Fiber < 1 g
Sugar 2 g
Protein 0 g

Asian Apricot Marinade

Servings 10
Serving Size 2 Tbsp
Calories 25
Fat 0 g
Saturated Fat 0 g
Cholesterol 0 mg
Sodium 200 mg
Carbohydrates 5 g
Fiber 0 g
Sugar 4 g
Protein < 1 g

Pick your protein, whether it is pork or chicken. Allow your protein to bathe for a few hours or just a few minutes depending on time available..

FourSide Jar

2 Tbsp rice vinegar
2 Tbsp tamari
2 Tbsp honey
¼ C water
1 Tbsp sesame oil
2 apricots, pitted and halved
½ clove garlic
1 chunk ginger root, peeled and approximately 1 tsp
1 chunk onion, approximately 1 Tbsp

Add ingredients to jar and secure lid. Select "Sauces".

Soups

Soups

Butternut Squash Soup

Take this soup for a spin and try one of the variations to enliven the taste buds.

Servings 6
Serving Size 1 cup
Calories 130
Fat 6 g
Saturated Fat 1 g
Cholesterol 0 mg
Sodium 125 mg
Carbohydrates 19 g
Fiber 5 g
Sugar 4 g
Protein 4 g

WildSide Jar
1 lg butternut squash, approximately 4-5 lbs
2 Tbsp olive oil, divided
1 carrot, approximately ½ C chopped
1 stalk celery, approximately ½ C chopped
1 onion, approximately ⅔ C chopped
⅛ tsp dried thyme
¼ tsp kosher salt
⅛ tsp ground black pepper
1 C water
2 (14 oz) cans low-sodium chicken broth

Preheat oven to 400°F. Cut large butternut squash in half lengthwise, pierce squash skin with fork, and remove seeds. Brush squash halves with 1 tablespoon oil and place flesh-side down in pan. Fill pan with ¼ cup water to prevent drying of squash. Bake until tender, approximately 45-60 minutes. Reserve one half of baked butternut squash for a future meal.

While squash is baking, heat 1 tablespoon oil in large pot. Sauté carrot, celery and onion for 2–3 minutes and then add thyme, salt and pepper. Cook until onion is translucent, another 2–3 minutes. Add water, cooked carrot, celery, and onion to jar and secure lid. Select "Batters". Pour pureed mirepoix back into large pot. Add one can of chicken broth to large pot. Bring to simmer. Scoop flesh from one squash half. Add second can of broth and squash flesh to jar and secure lid. Select "Soups". Pour into large pot, stir and allow all flavors to marry and simmer for a few minutes before serving.

For a Thai Twist, follow directions above and add 1 tablespoon red curry paste and ½ tablespoon ginger root to carrot, celery, and onion mixture. Cook until aromatic. Then when blending mirepoix mixture substitute ⅓ cup of water with ⅓ cup coconut milk.

For a Southwestern Spin, follow directions above and add ½ teaspoon cumin to carrot, celery and onion mixture. Garnish each soup with toasted butternut squash seeds, crumbled queso fresco and cilantro.

For a Dulcet Dip, follow directions above and add ¾ of a peeled and cored apple to carrot, celery, and onion mixture while sautéing. Before serving, add a little brie to bottom of soup bowl. Pour soup and garnish with remaining apple and toasted almond slices.

Sweet Potato Bisque

Servings 7
Serving Size 1 cup
Calories 120
Fat 3.5 g
Saturated Fat 0 g
Cholesterol 4 mg
Sodium 190 mg
Carbohydrates 18 g
Fiber 2 g
Sugar 7 g
Protein 5 g

This rich-hued root-vegetable soup is smooth and off the charts for your daily vitamin A intake.

WildSide Jar
1 Tbsp olive oil
1 medium onion, roughly chopped
1 clove garlic, roughly chopped
2 medium sweet potatoes, baked
3 C chicken broth
1 C low-fat milk
¼ tsp chili powder
¼ tsp ground cumin
⅛ tsp ground black pepper

Add oil to sauté pan and cook onions and garlic over medium heat until tender. Remove skin from baked sweet potatoes. Add broth, milk, seasonings, sauteed onions and garlic and baked sweet potatoes to jar and secure lid. Select "Soups" and serve.

Tomato Basil Soup

Servings 6
Serving Size 1 cup
Calories 140
Fat 7 g
Saturated Fat 4 g
Cholesterol 20 mg
Sodium 590 mg
Carbohydrates 18 g
Fiber 4 g
Sugar 4 g
Protein 5 g

Accompany this simply satisfying soup with crusty whole-grain bread for a light meal.

WildSide Jar
2 Tbsp butter
1 C chicken broth
3 C tomato juice, divided
4 C tomatoes, diced
10 fresh basil leaves
½ C half and half, warmed

Heat butter in large saucepan. While the butter heats, stir continuously until the butter begins to brown. Add broth and 2 cups tomato juice to saucepan. Add remaining tomato juice, diced tomatoes and basil leaves to jar and secure lid. Select "Whole Juice". Pour tomato basil blend into saucepan and simmer for 15–20 minutes. Remove from heat and cool slightly. Add half and half to sauce pan and stir. Serve and garnish with basil ribbons and cracked pepper.

Walnut Mushroom Soup

Servings 4
Serving Size 1 cup
Calories 180
Fat 13 g
Saturated Fat 1.5 g
Cholesterol 0 mg
Sodium 350 mg
Carbohydrates 9 g
Fiber 4 g
Sugar 2 g
Protein 8 g

A quick and delicious vegan cream of mushroom soup made creamy by the omega-3 loaded walnut. Just one ounce of walnuts offers over 2.5 grams of this essential fatty acid that our heart loves. Toast the walnuts for added depth of flavor.

FourSide Jar
1 Tbsp olive oil
1 medium onion, chopped
1 lb fresh mushrooms, cleaned, sliced and divided
½ tsp dried thyme
1 ½ C vegetable broth, divided
⅔ C almond or soy milk
½ C walnuts, toasted
¼ tsp kosher salt

Heat oil in pan over medium heat. Sauté onions and mushrooms, reserving 1 cup of mushrooms to blend with walnuts. Cook 5 minutes or until softened. Add 1 cup of broth and thyme to pan and bring to boil. Reduce heat and simmer. Add remaining ½ cup broth and 1 cup mushrooms, milk, walnuts, and salt to jar and secure lid. Select "Batters". Pour walnut mixture into pan. Allow soup to simmer for a few minutes for flavors to mingle and to thicken. Season with salt and pepper and garnish with croutons and serve.

Try adding ½ teaspoon sherry vinegar to lift the flavor.

Creamy Curry Carrot Soup

Mascarpone cheese, an Italian creamy cheese, helps to tone down the fusion of chillies, carrots and curry. Reduce the amount of curry paste for a milder flavor.

Either Jar

1 Tbsp olive oil
2 shallots, roughly chopped
1 clove garlic, quartered
¼ tsp kosher salt
4 medium carrots, roughly chopped, approximately 2 C
2 C chicken broth
1 Tbsp red curry paste
4 Tbsp mascarpone cheese, divided
1 Tbsp chives, chopped

Heat oil in deep saucepan and add shallots, garlic and salt and cook for 3–4 minutes. Add carrots and cook for 10 minutes. Add chicken broth and curry paste to jar and carefully add cooked carrots, shallots, and garlic. Secure lid and select "Soups". Pour blended soup back into deep saucepan and bring to simmer. Stir 2 tablespoon mascarpone cheese into soup. Serve soup and garnish with remaining mascarpone cheese and chives.

Toasted Almond and Broccoli Soup

A soothing vegetable soup made with pureed almonds to offer a touch of creaminess.

Both Jars

⅔ C almonds
3 C vegetable broth, low-sodium
4 C broccoli florets, steamed
2 zucchini, sliced and steamed
¼ tsp kosher salt
⅛ tsp ground black pepper

Preheat oven to 350°F. Add almonds to FourSide jar and secure lid. Press "Speed Up" to Speed 1, run cycle for 30 seconds and press "Pulse" to stop cycle. Spread coarse almond meal on cookie sheet and toast in preheated oven for 5–8 minutes, until toasted and aromatic. Set aside 3 tablespoons almonds for garnish. Add remaining ingredients to WildSide jar in order listed, including the toasted almonds, and secure lid. Select "Soups". Serve and garnish with ½ tablespoon toasted almond meal.

Tortilla Soup

A great soup for a quick supper. Pulse in corn kernels, black beans, tortilla chips or your favorite add-in for a chunky soup.

Either Jar

2 Roma tomatoes or 1 beefsteak tomato, quartered
½ large carrot
1" slice red pepper, approximately ⅓ C
¼ avocado, approximately ¼ C avocado flesh
1 chunk onion, approximately 2 Tbsp
1"x 1" chunk pepper jack cheese, approximately 1 oz
2 sprigs fresh cilantro
1 tsp no–salt herb seasoning
¾ tsp kosher salt
¾ tsp garlic powder
2 C warm water

Add ingredients to jar in order listed and secure lid. Select "Soups" and serve. For more texture, pulse in additional ingredients such as ½ cup tortilla chips, black beans, corn kernels, cheese, chicken or fresh tomato.

For Tomato Basil Soup, follow instructions as above but substitute 6 medium basil leaves for cilantro and add ½ tablespoon agave nectar.

Baked Potato Soup

Servings 3
Serving Size 1 ¼ cups
Calories 240
Fat 9 g
Saturated Fat 4.5 g
Cholesterol 30 mg
Sodium 600 mg
Carbohydrates 27 g
Fiber 2 g
Sugar 9 g
Protein 16 g

A creamy potato soup which includes all the toppings of a loaded baked potato. This soup is a whole meal and can be the centerpiece for a casual weekend dinner.

Either Jar

1 ¾ C milk, warmed
¼ C light sour cream
1 green onion, trimmed and halved
2 oz reduced fat cheddar cheese
¼ tsp kosher salt
⅛ tsp ground black pepper
2 large Yukon Gold potatoes, baked or boiled
3 slices bacon, cooked and divided

Add milk, sour cream, green onion, cheddar cheese, salt and pepper, and 1 baked potato to jar in order listed and secure lid. Select "Soups". Add the second potato and bacon and secure lid. Press "Pulse" 2–4 times to chop and incorporate ingredients for a chunky potato soup. Serve soup and garnish with desired baked potato toppings.

Gazpacho

Servings 4
Serving Size 1 cup
Calories 100
Fat 7 g
Saturated Fat 1 g
Cholesterol 0 mg
Sodium 310 mg
Carbohydrates 9 g
Fiber 2 g
Sugar 6 g
Protein 2 g

Chilled gazpacho is an ideal tonic for the hot days of summer.

Either Jar

1 ½ C tomato juice
1 beefsteak tomato, quartered
½ cucumber, peeled and quartered
½ small onion
½ green bell pepper, cored and seeded
2 Tbsp red wine vinegar
2 Tbsp olive oil
⅛ tsp kosher salt
⅛ tsp ground black pepper
⅛ tsp hot sauce

Add ingredients to jar in order listed and secure lid. Select "Soups". Chill or serve immediately.

Roasted Curried Cauliflower Soup

Smooth and silky soup great as an appetizer or for a light dinner. Garnish with chopped parsley.

Servings 5
Serving Size 1 ½ cups
Calories 100
Fat 6 g
Saturated Fat 1 g
Cholesterol 0 mg
Sodium 650 mg
Carbohydrates 12 g
Fiber 4 g
Sugar 5 g
Protein 4 g

WildSide Jar
1 head cauliflower, chopped into florets, approximately 6 C
1 onion, sliced into ¼" rings
2 Tbsp olive oil
1 ½ tsp curry powder
1 tsp kosher salt
3 C water
2 tsp Herbed Vegetable Broth Powder, see page 112

Preheat oven to 425°F. Toss the first 5 ingredients in a baking pan. Roast vegetables for 25 minutes. Add water and Herbed Vegetable Broth Powder to jar with 3 cups of roasted cauliflower and onions and secure lid. Press "Speed Up" to Speed 6. Pour 1 cup of soup into each bowl and top soup with approximately ½ cup of roasted vegetables.

Herbed Vegetable Broth Powder

Servings 48
Serving Size 1 tsp
Calories 5
Fat 0 g
Saturated Fat 0 g
Cholesterol 0 mg
Sodium 520 mg
Carbohydrates 1 g
Fiber 0 g
Sugar 0 g
Protein < 1 g

This vegetable bouillon powder is made with real ingredients and only has half the sodium of traditional broth recipes.

FourSide Jar

¾ C nutritional yeast
⅓ C sea salt
¼ C dried mushrooms
¼ C dried mixed vegetables
1 ½ Tbsp onion powder
1 Tbsp garlic powder
2 tsp dried parsley
1 tsp celery seed
1 tsp dried dill
1 tsp dried lemon zest
1 tsp dried thyme
1 tsp dried marjoram

Add ingredients to jar in order listed and secure lid. Press "Speed Up" to Speed 4 and run full cycle. Store in a closed container in a cool, dry place. Use 1 teaspoon per one cup water to make 1 cup broth.

Avocado Soup

Servings 6
Serving Size 1 cup
Calories 120
Fat 9
Sat Fat 2
Cholesterol 5 mg
Sodium 600 mg
Carbohydrates 8 g
Fiber 4 g
Sugar 3 g
Protein 3 g

This simple, creamy soup is delicious served cold and accompanied with a little scoop of ceviche to brighten up this appetizer.

WildSide Jar
4 C chicken broth
1 C milk
1 C water
2 Tbsp lime juice
2 ripe avocados, peeled and pitted
¼ C fresh cilantro leaves
½ serrano chile

Add ingredients to jar in order listed and secure lid. Select "Soups" and serve.

Beans and Greens Soup

Combine beans and greens for a quick and warming weeknight dinner. The greens in the soup provide your daily dose of vitamin C and also help enhance the absorption the non-heme iron in the beans.

Servings 5
Serving Size 1 cup
Calories 160
Fat 4 g
Saturated Fat 0 g
Cholesterol 0 mg
Sodium 600 mg
Carbohydrates 32 g
Fiber 9 g
Sugar 4 g
Protein 11 g

FourSide Jar 🅾

1 Tbsp olive oil
1 medium onion, roughly chopped
1 clove garlic, minced
2 C water, divided
2 tsp Herbed Vegetable Broth Powder, see page 112
4 C kale, approximately 6-8 leaves, ribs removed and roughly chopped
2 (15 oz) can white beans, drained, rinsed and divided
½ tsp crushed red pepper
¼ tsp ground cumin

Heat oil over medium-high heat in large sauté pan. Add onion and garlic and cook until tender, approximately 5 minutes. Add 1 cup water, herbed vegetable broth powder and kale to pan and cover. Cook until kale is wilted, approximately 5 minutes. While kale is softening, add remaining water, half of beans, crushed red pepper and cumin to jar. Select "Batters". Add bean blend and remaining whole beans to pan. Simmer for approximately 5 minutes and serve.

Substitute 2 cups low-sodium vegetable broth for 2 teaspoons Herbed Vegetable Broth Powder and 2 cups water.

Refreshing Berry Soup

Servings 6
Serving Size 1 ¼ cups
Calories 160
Fat 2 g
Saturated Fat 1 g
Cholesterol 3 mg
Sodium 85 mg
Carbohydrates 31 g
Fiber 6 g
Sugar 22 g
Protein 7 g

A sweet starter soup for any brunch or lunch with the ladies. Red raspberries make a bright garnish for the soup adding more fiber than sugar.

WildSide Jar
4 C strawberries
2 C low-fat vanilla yogurt
1 C low-fat milk, divided
⅓ C orange juice
6 Tbsp agave nectar, divided
1 tsp fresh lemon juice
2 C raspberries

Add strawberries, yogurt, ⅔ cup milk, orange juice and 4 tablespoon agave nectar to jar and secure lid. Select "Batters". Pour 1 cup soup into each of 6 bowls. Add remaining milk (⅓ cup), agave nectar (2 tablespoon), lemon juice and raspberries to jar and secure lid. Select "Batters". Drizzle and swirl ¼ cup raspberry blend over soup base and serve.

Try adding a lemon or orange zest to the strawberry or raspberry blend for a popping citrus flavor.

Meal Ideas

Meal Ideas

Sesame Flax Chicken

Servings 4
Serving Size 1 piece
Calories 260
Fat 10 g
Saturated Fat 1.5 g
Cholesterol 65 mg
Sodium 140 mg
Carbohydrates 11 g
Fiber 4 g
Sugar 1 g
Protein 31 g

Keep the fried chicken in the bucket and give this crusted chicken loaded with omega-3's a try. Feel free to toast the crumb mixture over a hot skillet for a few minutes to give it a little extra crunch and toasty flavor.

FourSide Jar

1 slice whole wheat bread, toasted and quartered
¼ C flaxseeds
3 Tbsp sesame seeds
2 Tbsp wheat germ
2 Tbsp dried parsley
¼ tsp crushed red pepper
4 (4 oz) chicken breast halves

Preheat oven to 400°F. Add ingredients except chicken to jar and secure lid. Press "Speed Up" to Speed 3, run for 35 seconds and press "Pulse" to stop cycle. Set an oven-safe cooling rack on a large baking sheet or jelly roll pan. Dip marinated or seasoned chicken breast halves in crumb mixture. Set breaded chicken on rack and spray with cooking oil. Bake for 15–20 minutes until done and juices run clear when chicken is pierced.

For a more moist and flavorful chicken, blend ½ cup soy sauce and 1 clove garlic. Marinate the chicken for 30 minutes in garlic soy sauce blend before breading.

Smashed Cauliflower and Cheese

Servings 5
Serving Size ¾ cup
Calories 90
Fat 4 g
Saturated Fat 2 g
Cholesterol 10 mg
Sodium 340 mg
Carbohydrates 9 g
Fiber 4 g
Sugar 5 g
Protein 7 g

Mashed cauliflower is a delicious, low-starch alternative to mashed potatoes. This cruciferous vegetable is an excellent source of vitamin C, containing almost as much vitamin C as oranges.

WildSide Jar

1 large head cauliflower, chopped into florets and steamed
2 Tbsp low-fat milk
¼ C low-fat sour cream
2 oz reduced fat cheddar cheese
½ tsp kosher salt
¼ tsp ground black pepper

Add ingredients to jar in order listed and secure lid. Press "Sauces" and serve.

Roasted Root Vegetable Mash

Servings 6
Serving Size ¾ cup
Calories 145
Fat 7 g
Saturated Fat 2 g
Cholesterol 7 mg
Sodium 460 mg
Carbohydrates 19 g
Fiber 3 g
Sugar 9 g
Protein 3 g

A little Neufchâtel cheese lends a savory and luxurious texture to this decadent and nutrient dense purée. Makes an ideal side dish for poultry.

WildSide Jar

2 sweet potatoes, cut into 1" pieces
4 carrots, peeled and cut into 1" slices
2 Tbsp olive oil
1 Tbsp brown sugar
¾ tsp kosher salt
1 ½ C vegetable broth, divided
2 oz Neufchâtel cheese

Heat oven to 375°F. Combine first 5 ingredients and spread evenly in 9"x 13" pan. Pour 1 cup broth over vegetables. Bake for 45–55 minutes, stirring occasionally, or until broth is absorbed and vegetables are tender and caramelized. Allow the vegetables to cool slightly before blending. Add roasted vegetables, remaining broth (½ cup) and the Neufchâtel cheese to jar and secure lid. Press "Sauces" and serve.

Note: Add more broth to puréed vegetables if needed for desired consistency.

Eggless Egg Salad

Servings 8
Serving Size ½ cup
Calories 220
Fat 21 g
Saturated Fat 1.5 g
Cholesterol 0 mg
Sodium 290 mg
Carbohydrates 3 g
Fiber < 1 g
Sugar < 1 g
Protein 6 g

Skip the cholesterol with this lunchtime and picnic-basket staple that is great as a sandwich spread, served on crackers or over a bed of greens.

WildSide Jar

1 C Vegan Mayo, see page 98
1 Tbsp prepared mustard
1 ½ tsp turmeric
1 tsp kosher salt
½ small red onion, quartered
1 celery stalk, quartered
1 clove garlic, quartered
14 oz extra firm tofu, drained and quartered

Add first 7 ingredients to jar and secure lid. Press "Pulse" 8–10 times until veggies are chopped. Add tofu and secure lid. Press "Pulse" until all ingredients are incorporated. Chill for several hours to allow flavors to meld.

Potato Spinach Cakes

Servings 7
Serving Size 2 cakes
Calories 200
Fat 8 g
Saturated Fat 3 g
Cholesterol 70 mg
Sodium 340 mg
Carbohydrates 26 g
Fiber 3 g
Sugar 4 g
Protein 9 g

Serve these moist and savory potato cakes with marinara sauce and salad for a light dinner.

WildSide Jar
2 slices whole wheat bread, toasted and quartered
10 oz spinach, approximately 6 C lightly packed
¾ C low-fat buttermilk
2 lg eggs
3 Yukon Gold potatoes, baked or boiled and quartered
2 cloves garlic, quartered
¼ tsp kosher salt
¼ tsp ground black pepper
¼ C Parmesan cheese
⅓ C feta cheese
1 ½ Tbsp olive oil, divided

Add toast to jar and secure lid. Press "Pulse" 6–8 times or until desired crumb size is reached. Set aside bread crumbs. In a large skillet, saute spinach in 1 ½ teaspoon olive oil until wilted. Add buttermilk, eggs, potatoes, garlic, salt, pepper, Parmesan cheese and bread crumbs to jar and secure lid. Select "Sauces". Using a spatula, incorporate sautéed spinach and feta cheese.

Preheat oven to 400°F. Heat 1 tablespoon oil in skillet or griddle. Scoop approximately ⅓ cup potato mixture onto skillet per cake. Cook each side until golden brown, 1–2 minutes. Place each cake onto baking sheet lined with parchment paper and bake for 10 minutes.

Grains

Grinding Grains

Cracking Grains: Cracking whole grains for hot cereals helps to shorten the cooking time and gives you all the nutritional benefits of the whole grain. Use the manual controls (Speed Up / Speed Down / Pulse) to crack grains. The grind will not be an even cracking but is semi-uniform. Crack grains to desired degree of fineness. If a finer cereal is desired, blend longer. Remember the longer the machine runs, the finer the consistency of the cereal, up to the point that it turns to flour.

	Whole Grains*	Cycle Speed	Blending Time
Buckwheat	2 C	2	4-5 seconds
Long-Grain White Rice	2 C	4	6-7 seconds
Long-Grain Brown Rice	2 C	4	6-7 seconds
Oat Groats	2 C	4	6-8 seconds
Wheat Berries	2 C	4	8-10 seconds
Pearled Barley	2 C	4	10-12 seconds

*These measurements are for use in your FourSide jar. For cracking grains in your WildSide jar, increase the amount of whole grains to 3 cups.

Cooking grains is similar to cooking rice. Add the dry grain in a pan with water or broth, bring to a boil and simmer until the liquid is absorbed. Grains can vary in cooking times depending on the grain variety and the age of the grain. If the grain is not as tender, simply add more water and continue cooking. If the grain seems done before all the liquid is absorbed, simply turn off the heat and drain excess water.

Whole Grain Flours

Grinding Grains: Grind fresh whole grains and legumes, packed with nutrients, and turn them into healthy whole grain flour. Making bread from start to finish is quick, easy, healthy and preservative-free, with a nuttier and fuller flavor. To lengthen the shelf life of freshly ground flour, store in an airtight container in the freezer and bring to room temperature before use.

Grains	Whole Grains*	Speed	Blending Time	Flour Yield
Amaranth	2 C	9	50 seconds	2 ¾ C
Long-Grain Brown Rice	2 C	9	50 seconds	2 ½ C
Buckwheat	2 C	5	50 seconds	2 ½ C
Dried Chickpeas	2 C	9	50 seconds	2 ½ C
Dried Fava Beans	2 C	7	50 seconds	2 C
Dried Green Lentils	2 C	7	50 seconds	2 ¼ C
Dried Soy Beans	2 C	7	50 seconds	2 ½ C
Dried White Beans	2 C	7	50 seconds	2 ¼ C
Flaxseeds	1 C	5	20 seconds	1 ½ C
Hulled Millet	2 C	7	50 seconds	2 ½ C
Oat Groats	2 C	9	30 seconds	3 C
Pearled Barley	2 C	9	50 seconds	3 C
Popcorn	2 C	7	50 seconds	2 ½ C (like fine polenta)
Quinoa	2 C	9	50 seconds	2 ½ C
Raw Almonds**	2 C	9	25 seconds	2 C
Rolled Oats	2 C	7	30 seconds	1 ¾ C
Rye Berries	2 C	9	50 seconds	2 ½ C
Spelt Berries	2 C	9	50 seconds	2 ½ C
Wheat Berries	2 C	9	50 seconds	2 ⅔ C
Long-Grain White Rice	2 C	7	50 seconds	2 C

*These measurements are for use in your FourSide jar. For grinding whole grain flours in your WildSide jar, increase the amount of whole grains to 3 cups.

** Do not over blend almond meal otherwise the nuts will release their oils and the result will be almond butter.

Note: When grinding hard grains, legumes or beans, it may pit the jar interior resulting in a "fogged" appearance. Please remember cosmetic alternations are not covered under your jar warranty.

Note: When making yeast breads, warm water for proofing yeast should be 110°F-115°F.

Quick Breads

Irish Soda Bread

Servings 8
Serving Size 1 slice
Calories 190
Fat 5 g
Saturated Fat 3 g
Cholesterol 15 mg
Sodium 340 mg
Carbohydrates 32 g
Fiber 4 g
Sugar 9 g
Protein 6 g

Traditional Irish Soda Bread is made with flour, baking soda, salt and soured milk. This recipe kicks up the flavor with orange zest and currants for a slightly sweet bread to be served at breakfast or brunch.

Wildside Jar

1 C low-fat buttermilk
3 Tbsp cold butter, cut into thirds
¼ C granulated sugar
2 (1"x 1") pieces orange zest
2 C whole white wheat flour, divided
1 ½ tsp baking powder
¾ tsp baking soda
½ tsp kosher salt
¾ C currants

Preheat oven to 375°F. Grease a 9" pie pan and set aside. Add buttermilk, butter, sugar and orange zest to jar and secure lid. Press "Pulse" 6-10 times until the butter is cut into coarse crumbs. Add half the flour with baking powder, baking soda and salt to jar and secure lid. Press "Pulse" 2-3 times. Add the remaining flour and currants to jar and secure lid. Press "Pulse" 4-6 times until all flour and currants are incorporated. Transfer dough by tilting jar over pie pan and using spatula to remove, spread and shape dough. Please note dough will not come to edges of pie pan. To score the loaf, use a serrated knife to lightly cut an X into the top of the loaf. Bake bread 40-50 minutes until toothpick inserted in center comes out clean. Cool and serve warm or at room temperature.

Cornbread

Servings 10
Serving Size 1 piece
Calories 180
Fat 6 g
Saturated Fat 1 g
Cholesterol 25 mg
Sodium 210 mg
Carbohydrates 27 g
Fiber 2 g
Sugar 8 g
Protein 5 g

Freeze any leftover cornbread to make cornbread croutons for your next Tex-Mex salad.

FourSide Jar

5 Tbsp butter, softened, divided
1 C buttermilk
2 eggs
½ C granulated sugar
¾ C all-purpose flour
1 C cornmeal
½ tsp kosher salt
1 tsp baking powder

Preheat oven to 400°F. Add 1 tablespoon butter to cast iron skillet and place in oven until butter melts. Remove pan from oven and swirl butter to coat bottom and sides. Add remaining ingredients to jar in order listed and secure lid. Select "Batters". Pour batter into hot skillet or greased pan. Bake for 15–20 minutes or until wooden toothpick inserted in center comes out clean. Serve warm.

For double corn bread, prepare as written except fold ½ cup corn into batter.

For corn muffins, prepare as written except omit 1 tablespoon butter used to grease skillet. Spoon batter into 12 greased muffin cups. Bake in 400° F oven for 15 minutes or until lightly browned and wooden toothpick inserted comes out clean.

Vegan Pumpkin Bread

Great texture and taste that is not too sweet. Whether it is for a crisp autumn day or rainy summer morning, this bread will please a crowd.

Servings 16
Serving Size 1 slice
Calories 140
Fat 4 g
Saturated Fat 0 g
Cholesterol 0 mg
Sodium 160 mg
Carbohydrates 27 g
Fiber 3 g
Sugar 13 g
Protein 3 g

FourSide Jar

1 ½ C whole wheat flour
½ C rolled oats
2 ½ tsp baking powder
½ tsp baking soda
½ tsp kosher salt
½ tsp ground cinnamon
¼ tsp ground allspice
¼ tsp ground nutmeg
½ C walnuts
½ C raisins
⅓ C water
⅓ C soy milk
¾ C maple syrup
1 C pumpkin purée
½ apple, cored and halved
1 ½ Tbsp flaxseeds

Preheat oven to 350°F. Add first 8 ingredients to jar and secure lid. Press "Pulse" 3–5 times to sift dry ingredients. Dump dry ingredients into a mixing bowl. Add walnuts to jar and secure lid. Press "Pulse" 3–5 times until walnuts are chopped and add to mixing bowl. Add raisins to mixing bowl. Add remaining ingredients to jar and secure lid. Select "Batters". Pour wet ingredients into mixing bowl and incorporate wet and dry ingredients. Pour batter into greased 8"x 4" loaf pan and bake for 45–50 minutes or until toothpick inserted in center comes out clean.

Peanut Butter Bread

This bread is great as a quick breakfast for the kids before they're off to school . To make your stomach smile, serve with strawberry freezer jam.

WildSide Jar

1 C fat-free milk

2 lg eggs

⅔ C granulated sugar

1 C peanut butter

1 tsp kosher salt

1 Tbsp baking powder

1 ¾ C all-purpose or whole white wheat flour

Preheat oven to 350°F. Add milk, eggs, sugar and peanut butter to jar and secure lid. Select "Batters". Add remaining ingredients and secure lid. Press "Pulse" 4–6 times or until flour is incorporated. Pour batter into greased 9"x 5" loaf pan. Bake for 50 minutes or until wooden toothpick inserted comes out clean.

For 4 mini loaves, divide batter among 4 mini loaf pans, bake for 30 minutes and share with friends and neighbors.

Pineapple Zucchini Bread

Servings 24
Serving Size 1 slice
Calories 150
Fat 5 g
Saturated Fat 0.5 g
Cholesterol 0 mg
Sodium 25 mg
Carbohydrates 24 g
Fiber 3 g
Sugar 12 g
Protein 3 g

A hearty and moist whole grain quick bread. This bread is quick to prepare and fills the house with a lovely aroma. For a wholesome treat for the neighbors, the recipe yields 6 mini loaves.

Wildside Jar
½ C walnuts
3 C all-purpose or whole white wheat flour
2 tsp baking soda
½ tsp baking powder
1 tsp kosher salt
1 Tbsp ground cinnamon
½ tsp ground nutmeg
3 lg eggs
1 ¼ C sucanat
1 apple, cored and quartered
2 tsp vanilla extract
1 ½ C pineapple chunks
1 medium zucchini, quartered

Preheat oven to 350˚F. Add walnuts, flour, baking soda and powder, salt, cinnamon and nutmeg to jar and secure lid. Press "Speed Up" to Speed 1 and allow full cycle to run. Dump dry ingredients into mixing bowl. Add eggs, sucanat, apple and vanilla to jar and secure lid. Select "Batters". Add pineapple chunks and zucchini to jar and secure lid. Press "Pulse" 15-20 times until pineapple and zucchini is finely graded. Pour batter into mixing bowl. Using a spatula, incorporate all ingredients and pour into 2 – 8"x 4" greased loaf pans. Bake for 50–60 minutes or wooden toothpick inserted in center comes out clean.

Yeast Breads

WildSide Whole Wheat Bread

Servings 16
Serving Size 1 slice
Calories 90
Fat 1.5 g
Saturated Fat 0 g
Cholesterol 0 mg
Sodium 125 mg
Carbohydrates 17 g
Fiber 3 g
Sugar 2 g
Protein 4 g

The secret to whole wheat bread is keeping the dough soft, just stiff enough to handle. The WildSide jar forms a nice soft dough ball ready to rise and bake.

WildSide Jar
1 C warm water
1 Tbsp dry active yeast
1 ½ Tbsp honey
1 tsp kosher salt
1 Tbsp fresh lemon juice
1 ½ Tbsp vegetable oil
2 ½ Tbsp vital wheat gluten
2 ⅔ C whole white wheat flour, divided

Add water, yeast and honey to jar and secure lid. Press "Pulse" 2 times. Allow the yeast to proof for 5–10 minutes. Add kosher salt, lemon juice, oil and gluten to jar and secure lid. Press "Pulse" 2 times. Add ⅓ of flour to jar and secure lid. Press "Pulse" 1 time. Add another ⅓ of flour and secure lid. Press "Pulse" 3–5 times. Add the last ⅓ of flour and secure lid. Press "Pulse" 8–10 times until all flour is incorporated and dough ball forms.

Preheat oven to 350°F. Allow dough to rest in jar for 10–15 minutes. Dump dough ball onto oiled surface and shape loaf. Place shaped loaf, seam side down, into 9"x 5" greased, loaf pan. Cover loaf pan and allow dough to rise for 20 minutes in a warm place or until dough has topped the pan by approximately one inch. Bake for approximately 22–25 minutes until done. Remove bread from pan and allow it to cool on a wire rack before slicing.

If you have wheat berries on hand and want to make your own flour, blend 2 cups wheat berries on speed 9 for full cycle. Set aside the freshly ground flour until after proofing of yeast.

FourSide Whole Wheat Bread

Nothing beats the aroma of freshly baked bread. Try this simple and straightforward method to make 100% whole wheat homemade bread.

Servings 12
Serving Size 1 slice
Calories 80
Fat 1.5 g
Saturated Fat 0 g
Cholesterol 0 mg
Sodium 100 mg
Carbohydrates 15 g
Fiber 3 g
Sugar 2 g
Protein 4 g

FourSide Jar
⅔ C warm water
2 tsp dry active yeast
1 Tbsp honey
¾ tsp kosher salt
1 Tbsp fresh lemon juice
1 Tbsp vegetable oil
1 ¾ Tbsp vital wheat gluten
1 ¾ C whole white wheat flour

Add water, yeast and honey to jar and secure lid. Press "Pulse" 2 times. Allow the yeast to proof for 5–10 minutes. Preheat oven to 350°F. Add kosher salt, lemon juice, oil and gluten to jar and secure lid. Press "Pulse" 1 time. Add ⅓ of flour to jar and secure lid. Press "Pulse" 2 times. Add next ⅓ of flour and secure lid. Press "Pulse" 4–6 times. Add last ⅓ of flour and secure lid. Press "Pulse" 8–10 times until flour is incorporated and dough ball forms.

Allow dough to rest in jar for 10-15 minutes. Dump dough ball onto oiled surface and shape loaf. Place shaped loaf, seam side down, into 8"x 4" greased loaf pan. Cover loaf pan and allow dough to rise for 20 minutes in a warm place or until dough has topped the pan by approximately one inch. Bake for 18–20 minutes until done. Remove bread from pan and allow it to cool on a wire rack before slicing.

If you have wheat berries on hand and would like to make your own flour, blend 1 ⅓ cups of wheat berries on Speed 9 for full cycle. Set aside the freshly ground wheat flour until after proofing the yeast.

Half and Half Bread

○ ○

Servings 16
Serving Size 1 slice
Calories 90
Fat 1 g
Saturated Fat 0 g
Cholesterol 0 mg
Sodium 130 mg
Carbohydrates 18 g
Fiber 2 g
Sugar 2 g
Protein 3 g

This recipe uses half all-purpose flour and half whole wheat flour for a slightly lighter loaf.

WildSide Jar
1 ¼ C warm water
1 Tbsp dry active yeast
2 Tbsp honey
1 ⅓ C all-purpose flour
1 ⅓ C whole white wheat flour
1 tsp kosher salt
1 Tbsp fresh lemon juice
2 Tbsp vegetable oil

Preheat oven to 350°F. Add water, yeast and honey to jar and secure lid. Press "Pulse" 2 times. Allow the yeast to proof for 5–10 minutes. Combine flours and set aside. Add salt, lemon juice and oil to jar and secure lid. Press "Pulse" 2 times. Add ⅓ of flour to jar and secure lid. Press "Pulse" 2 times. Add next ⅓ of flour and secure lid. Press "Pulse" 4–6 times. Add last of flour and secure lid. Press "Pulse" 8–10 times until all flour is incorporated and dough ball forms.

Allow dough to rest in jar for 10–15 minutes. Dump dough ball onto oiled surface and shape loaf. Place shaped loaf, seam side down, into 9"x 5" greased loaf pan. Cover loaf pan and allow dough to rise for 20 minutes in a warm place or until dough has topped the pan by approximately one inch. Bake for approximately 22–25 minutes until done. Remove bread from pan and allow it to cool on a wire rack before slicing.

For Oat Bread, as you add the flour, reduce all-purpose flour to 1 ¼ cups. During the second addition of flour, add ¾ cup rolled oats and continue following instructions accordingly.

For Buttermilk Bread, substitute the water with warm buttermilk and oil with butter. Increase all-purpose flour and whole white wheat flour to 1 ½ cups When adding in the salt, lemon juice and butter, add 1 egg and ¼ teaspoon of baking soda. Continue and follow instructions accordingly.

Pumpernickel Bread

A lighter crumb version to the original, dense German bread. Try this bread with egg or chicken salad for perfect picnic sandwiches.

Servings 16
Serving Size 1 slice
Calories 120
Fat 2 g
Saturated Fat 0 g
Cholesterol 0 mg
Sodium 125 mg
Carbohydrates 23 g
Fiber 3 g
Sugar 4 g
Protein 5 g

WildSide Jar
1 C whole wheat flour
1 C rye flour
1 C all-purpose flour
2 Tbsp cocoa powder
1 Tbsp vital wheat gluten
1 tsp kosher salt
1 C warm water
1 Tbsp dry active yeast
1 Tbsp honey
¼ C molasses
2 Tbsp vegetable oil
1 tsp fresh lemon juice

Add first 6 ingredients to jar in order listed and secure lid. Press "Pulse" 3–5 times to mix and sift dry ingredients. Set dry ingredients aside. Add water, yeast and honey to jar and secure lid. Press "Pulse" 2 times. Allow the yeast to proof 5–10 minutes. Add molasses, oil and lemon juice to jar and secure lid. Press "Pulse" 2 times. Add ⅓ of dry ingredients to jar and secure lid. Press "Pulse" 2–3 times. Add next ⅓ of dry ingredients to jar and secure lid. Press "Pulse" 4-6 times. Add the last ⅓ of dry ingredients to jar and secure lid. Press "Pulse" 6–8 times until all flour is incorporated and a dough ball forms.

Allow dough to rest in jar for 10–15 minutes. Dump dough ball onto oiled surface and shape loaf. Place shaped loaf, seam side down, into 9"x 5" greased loaf pan. Cover loaf pan and allow dough to rise for 20 minutes in a warm place or until dough has topped the pans by approximately one inch. Bake for 22–25 minutes until done. Remove bread from pan and allow it to cool on a wire rack before slicing.

Multi-Grain Bread

Try different seeds and grains such as quinoa, sesame, flaxseed, spelt and teff for a varying nutritional profile. Look for many of these grains and seeds in the bulk section at your local health food store to purchase the amount needed.

WildSide Jar

¾ C wheat berries*
2 Tbsp millet
2 Tbsp barley
2 Tbsp buckwheat
2 Tbsp brown rice
¼ C rye flour
¼ C cornmeal
¼ C rolled oats
1 ¼ C warm water
1 Tbsp dry active yeast
2 Tbsp honey
1 tsp kosher salt
1 tsp fresh lemon juice
1 Tbsp vegetable oil
3 Tbsp vital wheat gluten
¼ C sunflower seeds
1 C all-purpose flour

Preheat oven to 350°F. Add first 8 ingredients to jar and secure lid. Press "Speed Up" to Speed 9 and run full cycle. Set freshly milled flour aside. Add water, yeast and honey to jar and secure lid. Press "Pulse" 2 times. Allow the yeast to proof for 5–10 minutes. Add salt, lemon juice, oil, gluten, sunflower seeds and all-purpose flour to jar and secure lid. Press "Pulse" 2–3 times. Add ½ of whole grain flour to jar and secure lid. Press "Pulse" 4–6 times. Add remaining whole grain flour and secure lid. Press "Pulse" 6–8 times until all flour is incorporated and a dough ball forms.

Allow dough to rest in jar for 10–15 minutes. Dump dough ball onto oiled surface and shape loaf. Place shaped loaf, seam side down, into 9"x 5" greased loaf pan. Allow dough to rise for 20 minutes in a warm place or until dough has topped the pan by approximately one inch. Bake for approximately 22–25 minutes until done. Remove bread from pan and allow it to cool on a wire rack.

*If you do not have wheat berries on hand, replace with 1 cup whole wheat flour. Do not add whole wheat flour to jar when milling the various grains; instead add whole wheat flour when pulsing in flours to make dough.

Pizza, Pretzels, Pita or Cinnamon Rolls

Servings 8
Serving Size 1 piece
Calories 130
Fat 2.5 g
Saturated Fat 0 g
Cholesterol 0 mg
Sodium 100 mg
Carbohydrates 25 g
Fiber 4 g
Sugar 2 g
Protein 5 g

Even if pizza can't appear with the wave of a wand, it can with the push of a button. This versatile dough is quick, easy and great for pretzels, pita bread and cinnamon rolls with a touch of whole grain goodness.

WildSide Jar

¾ C warm water
1 Tbsp dry active yeast
1 Tbsp honey
1 C all-purpose flour
1 C whole white wheat flour
1 Tbsp vegetable oil
½ tsp kosher salt

Add water, yeast and honey to jar and secure lid. Press "Pulse" 1–2 times and allow yeast to proof 5-10 minutes. Combine all-purpose and whole wheat flour in separate bowl. Add oil, salt and ⅓ of flour to jar and secure lid. Press "Pulse" 2 times. Add next ⅓ of flour to jar and secure lid. Press "Pulse" 3–5 times. Add remaining flour and secure lid. Press "Pulse" 8–10 times until all flour is incorporated and a dough ball forms.

Allow dough to rise in jar with lid secure until doubled. Preheat oven to 450°F and heat baking stone or pan in oven. Roll out dough on a well oiled or floured surface. Place rolled-out dough on a paddle, thin cutting board or on a cookie sheet dusted with cornmeal. Cover dough with sauce and favorite toppings. Slide pizza from cornmeal covered surface by wiggling it gently onto the heated baking stone. Bake in oven until golden brown, approximately 8-12 minutes. When pizza is done, remove from oven and allow to cool 3-5 minutes before slicing.

For 100% whole wheat dough, omit all-purpose flour and use 2 cups whole white wheat flour.

For garlic herb pizza dough, pulse in 1 teaspoon dried basil, 1 teaspoon dried oregano and ¼ teaspoon garlic powder after proofing yeast and before adding flour.

For Pretzels, after rising the dough, form 8 two-foot ropes and twist into pretzel shapes. In a large pot bring to boil a gallon of water. Add ¼ cup baking soda to boiling water. Carefully drop the shaped pretzels, one at a time, into the boiling water and leave for approximately 30 seconds. Remove pretzels, place them on a lined baking sheet, brush them with beaten egg yolk and water and sprinkle with coarse salt. Bake in 450°F until brown, approximately 7-10 minutes.

For Pita Bread, after rising the dough, preheat oven to 500°F with rack at bottom of oven. Place baking stone or pan on bottom rack. Divide dough into 6 dough balls. Let sit covered for 10 minutes. Roll out each ball of dough into circles about 6-7" in diameter and ¼" thickness. Bake each pita for 3-5 minutes until the pita puffs up. Turn over and bake for 2 minutes. Remove each pita from baking stone or pan and add additional pitas for baking.

For Cinnamon Rolls, substitute milk for water and in place of 1 tablespoon oil add 2 tablespoons softened butter. Follow basic recipe instructions. After dough rises, roll out dough on oiled surface to 12"x 18" rectangle. Brush dough with ½ tablespoon melted butter. Sprinkle ½ cup brown sugar and ½ tablespoon ground cinnamon over the dough leaving ½" border along top 12" edge. Roll the dough into a tight cylinder and pinch the seam closed. Using a serrated knife, slice into 2" rolls; yielding 6 rolls. Arrange rolls cut side down and cover to rise for 20 minutes. Preheat oven to 350°F. Bake rolls for 16-18 minutes or until golden brown. Frost and serve.

Optional Cinnamon Roll Frosting:
2 oz Neufchâtel cheese
¼ C milk
1 C powdered sugar

Add ingredients to FourSide jar in order listed and secure lid. Press "Pulse" 4–6 times until blended.

Quick Yeast Rolls

◉

Servings 12
Serving Size 1 roll
Calories 150
Fat 3 g
Saturated Fat 1.5 g
Cholesterol 25 mg
Sodium 170 mg
Carbohydrates 27 g
Fiber 0 g
Sugar 5 g
Protein 5 g

No need to knead. This recipe gives you piping hot yeast rolls in less than 45 minutes without the kneading and shaping.

WildSide Jar

¾ C milk, warmed
3 Tbsp sugar
1 Tbsp dry active yeast
2 Tbsp butter, melted
1 tsp kosher salt
1 lg egg
2 ⅔ C all-purpose flour, divided

Preheat oven to 400°F. Add milk, sugar and yeast to jar and secure lid. Press "Pulse" 2 times. Allow the yeast to proof for 5–10 minutes. Add butter, salt, egg and ⅓ of flour to jar and secure lid. Press "Pulse" 2–3 times. Add next ⅓ of flour and secure lid. Press "Pulse" 3–5 times. Add remaining flour and secure lid. Press "Pulse" 8–10 times until all flour is incorporated and a dough ball forms.

Allow dough to rest in jar with lid secure until doubled. Grease a muffin tin. Dump dough ball onto oiled surface and divide into 12 dough balls. Place individual dough balls into muffin cups. Cover and let rise for 15 minutes or until dough rounds over each muffin cup. Bake for 12-14 minutes until done.

For Whole-Grain Dinner Rolls, substitute half of the all-purpose flour with whole wheat flour.

For Onion Herb Dinner Rolls, add 1 tablespoon dried minced onion and 2 teaspoons of dried herbs to jar when adding butter, salt, eggs and ⅓ of flour.

Gluten-Free

Gluten-Free (GF) Baking Mix

Servings 26
Serving Size ¼ cup
Calories 160
Fat 0 g
Saturated Fat 0 g
Cholesterol 0 mg
Sodium 5 mg
Carbohydrates 36 g
Fiber 2 g
Sugar 0 g
Protein 3 g

Many gluten-free items have a long list of ingredients. Keep this mix on hand so you can whip up breakfast or a snack anytime.

FourSide Jar
2 C white rice
1 C gluten-free rolled oats
2 C cornstarch
1 ½ C tapioca starch

Add white rice to jar and secure lid. Press "Speed Up" to Speed 9 and run full cycle. Add white rice flour to large bowl or zip-tip bag. Add oats to jar and secure lid. Press "Speed Up" to Speed 7, run cycle for 20 seconds and press "Pulse" to stop cycle. Add oat flour to white rice flour. Add the starches to the bowl or bag and incorporate all ingredients. Store gluten-free flour mix in the refrigerator or freezer and let it come to room temperature before use.

GF Chocolate Chip Cookies

Servings 24
Serving Size 1 cookie
Calories 130
Fat 6 g
Saturated Fat 4 g
Cholesterol 20 mg
Sodium 120 mg
Carbohydrates 19 g
Fiber 0 g
Sugar 10 g
Protein 1 g

A delicious gluten-free cookie that even "gluten eaters" will love.

FourSide Jar
1 ¾ C Gluten-Free Baking Mix, see page 142
1 ½ tsp xanthan gum
1 tsp baking soda
1 tsp baking powder
½ tsp kosher salt
¾ C chocolate chips
½ C butter, softened
1 lg egg
½ C brown sugar, packed
1 tsp vanilla extract

Preheat oven to 375°F. Add baking mix, xanthan gum, baking soda, baking powder and salt to jar and secure lid. Press "Pulse" 3–5 times to sift dry ingredients. Dump dry ingredients into a mixing bowl. Add chocolate chips to mixing bowl. Add remaining ingredients to jar and secure lid. Select "Batters". Pour wet ingredients into mixing bowl. Using a spatula, incorporate wet and dry ingredients. Drop by spoonfuls onto cookie sheet and bake for 6–8 minutes.

GF Pumpkin Quick Bread

Servings 12
Serving Size ¾" slice
Calories 170
Fat 7 g
Saturated Fat 1 g
Cholesterol 35 mg
Sodium 210 mg
Carbohydrates 26 g
Fiber 2 g
Sugar 10 g
Protein 3 g

A sweet autumn treat packed with vitamin A. Makes a great snack for a beautiful autumn day at the park!

WildSide Jar
¼ C canola oil
2 lg eggs
¼ C maple syrup
1 C pumpkin purée
¾ C brown sugar, packed
1 ½ C Gluten-Free Baking Mix, see page 142
1 tsp xanthan gum
1 tsp baking soda
1 tsp ground cinnamon
1 tsp vanilla extract
½ tsp kosher salt
½ tsp ground ginger
¼ tsp ground cloves

Preheat oven to 325°F. Add ingredients to jar in order listed and secure lid. Press "Pulse" 8-10 times until ingredients are incorporated. Pour batter into a greased 9"x 5" loaf pan. Bake for 50 minutes until done.

GF Pancakes

Servings 3
Serving Size 2 pancakes
Calories 320
Fat 12 g
Saturated Fat 1.5 g
Cholesterol 70 mg
Sodium 230 mg
Carbohydrates 48 g
Fiber 3 g
Sugar 7 g
Protein 8 g

Whether it is for breakfast-in-bed or a quick weekday breakfast, enjoy these fluffy and tender pancakes.

FourSide Jar

¾ C milk
1 Tbsp oil
1 Tbsp honey
1 lg egg
1 C Gluten-Free Baking Mix, see page 142
1 tsp baking powder
½ tsp xanthan gum
¼ tsp baking soda

Add ingredients to jar in order listed and secure lid. Select "Batters". Let batter rest for a few minutes. Heat griddle and pour ¼ cup batter per pancake onto heated and greased griddle or other pan. Cook until bubbles break the top surface of the pancake and the underside is golden brown. Flip and cook until done. Repeat with remaining batter. Serve immediately or keep warm in the oven at 200°F loosely wrapped in foil.

GF Muffins

This gluten-free goodie is a basic muffin recipe with bananas and blueberries.

Servings 12
Serving Size 1 muffin
Calories 160
Fat 3 g
Saturated Fat 0 g
Cholesterol 20 mg
Sodium 220 mg
Carbohydrates 32 g
Fiber 2 g
Sugar 10 g
Protein 3 g

FourSide Jar
⅔ C milk
⅓ C honey
1 whole egg and 1 egg white
1 ripe banana
2 C Gluten-Free Baking Mix, see page 142
1 tsp baking soda
1 tsp baking powder
1 tsp xanthan gum
1 tsp vanilla extract
½ tsp kosher salt
1 C blueberries

Preheat oven to 350°F. Add ingredients to jar, except blueberries, in order listed and secure lid. Select "Batters". Fold in blueberries using a spatula. Pour batter into a greased muffin tin or a tin lined with paper cups. Bake 16–18 minutes until done.

Quinoa Corn Muffins

Servings 12
Serving Size 1 muffin
Calories 140
Fat 6 g
Saturated Fat 1 g
Cholesterol 20 mg
Sodium 170 mg
Carbohydrates 19 g
Fiber 1 g
Sugar 7 g
Protein 3 g

Those keen on quinoa know this little ancient seed is a complete protein and great for gluten-free cooking and baking. This simple muffin recipe containing honey adds a gentle touch of sweetness.

FourSide Jar
1 whole egg and 1 egg white
⅔ C milk
¼ C vegetable oil
¼ C honey
4 tsp baking powder
½ tsp kosher salt
⅔ C cornmeal
⅔ C quinoa flour

Preheat oven to 400°F. Add first 4 ingredients in order listed and secure lid. Press "Pulse" 4–6 times. Add remaining ingredients and secure lid. Press "Pulse" 4–6 times. Allow batter to rest for a few minutes. Pour batter into a greased muffin tin or a tin lined with paper cups. Bake 15–17 minutes until done.

Egg Bread

This recipe makes two loaves and is great for sandwich bread, rolls or breadsticks.

Servings 24
Serving Size 1 slice
Calories 100
Fat 2 g
Saturated Fat 0 g
Cholesterol 35 mg
Sodium 140 mg
Carbohydrates 19 g
Fiber 0 g
Sugar 2 g
Protein 2 g

WildSide Jar
2 C white rice
1 ½ tsp kosher salt
1 Tbsp xanthan gum
1 ¾ C tapioca starch
1 ⅔ C warm water
¼ C honey
1 ½ Tbsp dry active yeast
¼ C canola oil
1 tsp apple cider vinegar
3 whole eggs and 2 egg yolks

Preheat oven to 375°F. Add rice, salt and xanthan gum to jar and secure lid. Press "Speed Up" to Speed 9 and run full cycle. Add tapioca starch to jar and secure lid. Press "Pulse" 2-3 times to incorporate and sift dry ingredients. Set dry ingredients aside. Add water, honey, and yeast to jar and secure lid. Press "Pulse" 2 times and allow yeast to proof for 5–10 minutes. Add oil, vinegar and eggs to jar and secure lid. Press "Pulse" 3 times. Remove vented gripper lid insert and press "Speed Up" to Speed 1. Add approximately ¾ of dry ingredients over duration of cycle. Add last of dry ingredients and secure lid. Press "Pulse" 6–8 times until all dry ingredients are incorporated (may need to use spatula to scrape sides and incorporate remaining flour). Divide dough between two greased 9"x 5" loaf pans. Cover and let rise for 25–30 minutes in a warm place or until dough has topped the pan by approximately one inch. Bake for 30-35 minutes.

For Breadsticks, divide the dough in half. Place one half in the loaf pan, let rise and bake according to instructions. Place the other half in a zip-top bag and snip off the bottom corner of bag. Squeeze out dough in shape of breadsticks onto a greased baking pan. Cover and rise for 15 minutes. Bake at 350°F for 13–15 minutes until done.

Millet Brown Rice Bread

The mighty millet isn't just for the birds; this loaf is gluten-free, egg-free and dairy-free.

Servings 12
Serving Size 1 slice
Calories 100
Fat 0.5 g
Saturated Fat 0 g
Cholesterol 0 mg
Sodium 110 mg
Carbohydrates 22 g
Fiber 1 g
Sugar 3 g
Protein 2 g

Either Jar

⅔ C millet
½ C brown rice, scant ½ C
1 ¼ C warm water
¼ C sugar
1 Tbsp dry active yeast
½ C potato starch
⅓ C tapioca starch
⅓ C corn starch
2 tsp xanthan gum
2 tsp egg replacer
1 tsp kosher salt

Preheat oven to 350°F. Add millet and brown rice to jar and secure lid. Press "Speed Up" to Speed 9 and run full cycle. Set flour aside. Add water, sugar and yeast to jar and secure lid. Press "Pulse" 2 times and allow yeast to proof for 5–10 minutes. Add the remaining ingredients, including millet and brown rice flour, and secure lid. Select "Batters". Tilt jar over loaf pan and place dough into greased 8"x 4" loaf pan. Cover and let rise for 20 minutes in a warm place or until dough has topped the pan by approximately ½ inch. Bake for 25–30 minutes.

Millet Irish Soda Bread

Servings 12
Serving Size 1 piece
Calories 190
Fat 6 g
Saturated Fat 2 g
Cholesterol 45 mg
Sodium 330 mg
Carbohydrates 33 g
Fiber 2 g
Sugar 13 g
Protein 3 g

It doesn't have to be St. Patty's day to enjoy this Irish Soda Bread. This moist and flavorful version has a touch of orange and cranberries.

WildSide Jar
¾ C milk
1"x 1" piece orange zest
¼ C butter, softened
¼ C honey
½ tsp apple cider vinegar
2 lg eggs
1 C millet flour
½ C sorghum flour
½ C potato starch
2 tsp xanthan gum
1 ½ tsp baking powder
1 tsp baking soda
1 tsp kosher salt
1 C dried cranberries

Preheat oven to 350°F. Add milk, zest, butter, honey, vinegar and eggs to jar and secure lid. Select "Batters". Add remaining ingredients, except cranberries, and secure lid. Select "Batters". Fold in dried cranberries using spatula. Pour batter into a greased 9" pie pan and using a sharp knife, slice a criss-cross into the dough. Bake for 35-40 minutes until done.

Desserts

Baked

Best Blender Brownies

Step out of the box and give this recipe a try for a nice, rich, fudgy brownie.

Servings 15
Serving Size 1 piece
Calories 270
Fat 15 g
Saturated Fat 7 g
Cholesterol 65 mg
Sodium 80 mg
Carbohydrates 36 g
Fiber 2 g
Sugar 27 g
Protein 3 g

WildSide Jar
¾ **C butter, melted**
⅔ **C semi-sweet chocolate chips**
3 **lg eggs**
½ **C cocoa powder**
1 ½ **C sugar**
1 **tsp vanilla extract**
⅞ **C all-purpose flour**

Preheat oven to 350°F. Add butter and chocolate chips to jar. Secure lid and select "Batters". Add eggs, cocoa, sugar and vanilla to jar and secure lid. Press "Pulse" 3–5 times. Add the flour and secure lid. Press "Pulse" 3–5 times or until flour is incorporated. Use a spatula to scrape down the sides of jar. Pour into greased 9"x 9" or 11"x 7" pan. Bake for 30 minutes or until wooden toothpick inserted in center comes out clean.

For nut lovers, fold 1 cup chopped walnuts or pecans into batter.
For chocolate lovers, fold 1 cup semi-sweet chocolate chips into batter.

Quick Chocolate Frosting

These five ingredients whip up a tempting chocolate frosting that beats anything from the store that has been made with 15 plus ingredients.

Servings 16
Serving Size 2 Tbsp
Calories 120
Fat 6 g
Saturated Fat 4 g
Cholesterol 15 mg
Sodium 45 mg
Carbohydrates 17 g
Fiber < 1 g
Sugar 16 g
Protein < 1 g

FourSide Jar
⅓ **C milk**
½ **C butter, softened**
1 **tsp vanilla extract**
½ **C cocoa powder**
2 ½ **C powdered sugar**

Add ingredients to jar in order listed and secure lid. Press "Pulse" 4–6 times. Use a spatula to scrape sides and move ingredients toward center of jar and secure lid. Press "Pulse" 3–5 times. Use immediately or store in covered container in refrigerator.

Peanut Butter Brownies

Servings 35
Serving Size 1 bar
Calories 200
Fat 11 g
Saturated Fat 5 g
Cholesterol 30 mg
Sodium 125 mg
Carbohydrates 20 g
Fiber 2 g
Sugar 14 g
Protein 4 g

While not low-fat, these scrumptiously sweet brownies are 100% whole grain, but no one will know.

WildSide Jar

2 C rolled oats
2 C whole wheat pastry flour
1 tsp baking powder
½ tsp kosher salt
1 C butter, softened
2 lg eggs
1 C creamy peanut butter
2 tsp vanilla extract
1 C brown sugar
1 C granulated sugar

Quick Chocolate Frosting Recipe, see page 153

Preheat oven to 350°F. Measure the oats and add to mixing bowl. Add whole wheat pastry flour, baking powder and salt to jar and secure lid. Press "Pulse" 2–3 times to sift dry ingredients. Add dry ingredients to mixing bowl. Add the remaining ingredients to jar in order listed and secure lid. Select "Batters". Add peanut butter batter to mixing bowl and incorporate with dry ingredients. Press stiff peanut butter batter into jelly roll pan. Bake for 20 minutes until done. While brownies are baking, prepare the Quick Chocolate Frosting. Allow bars to cool, then frost.

Ultimate Chocolate Chip Cookie

Servings 12
Serving Size 2 cookies
Calories 260
Fat 14 g
Saturated Fat 6 g
Cholesterol 30 mg
Sodium 170 mg
Carbohydrates 31 g
Fiber 3 g
Sugar 18 g
Protein 4 g

Legend says Mrs. Wakefield, owner of the Toll House Inn, whipped up a batch of her cookies and found herself without the needed ingredient and substituted it for a chopped semi-sweet chocolate bar. Now this cookie is a staple in every baker's repertoire and this recipe is a twist on the traditional made with whole grains and flaxseeds.

FourSide Jar

⅔ C rolled oats
2 Tbsp flaxseeds
1 C whole white wheat flour
½ tsp baking soda
½ tsp kosher salt
¼ C canola oil
¼ C butter, softened
1 lg egg
⅓ C granulated sugar
⅓ C brown sugar
1 tsp vanilla extract
1 C semi-sweet chocolate chips

Preheat oven to 350°F. Add oats and flaxseeds to the jar and secure lid. Press "Speed Up" to Speed 3, run for 25 seconds and press "Pulse" to stop. Stir ground oats and flaxseed and add whole wheat flour, soda and salt to jar and secure lid. Press "Pulse" 3–5 times to sift dry ingredients. Add dry ingredients into a mixing bowl. Add the next 6 ingredients to the jar and secure lid. Select "Batters". Add wet ingredients and chocolate chips to mixing bowl and incorporate wet and dry ingredients. Drop cookie dough by rounded tablespoonfuls onto a baking sheet. Bake for 8–10 minutes until done.

For a lower fat version, substitute cinnamon applesauce for the oil.

Chocolate Buttermilk Cake

Known to some as Texas Sheet Cake, but then who wouldn't want to claim this moist and chocolatey cake? This version uses prunes to replace half of the butter.

Servings 30
Serving Size 1 piece
Calories 180
Fat 7 g
Saturated Fat 4 g
Cholesterol 30 mg
Sodium 135 mg
Carbohydrates 30 g
Fiber 1 g
Sugar 21 g
Protein 2 g

WildSide Jar
1 C water
1 C low-fat buttermilk
½ C prunes, approximately 8-10
2 lg eggs
⅓ C cocoa powder
1 tsp kosher salt
½ C butter, softened
1 ¾ C granulated sugar
1 tsp baking soda
1 tsp ground cinnamon
2 C all-purpose flour

Quick Chocolate Frosting, see page 153

Preheat oven to 375°F. Add water, buttermilk, prunes and eggs to jar and secure lid. Select "Batters". Add next 4 ingredients and secure lid. Select "Batters". Add remaining ingredients and secure lid. Press "Pulse" 8–10 times until flour is incorporated. Pour onto greased jelly roll pan. Bake for 18–20 minutes until done. While the cake is baking, prepare the Quick Chocolate Frosting. Spread frosting over warm cake.

If you do not have any buttermilk on hand, substitute sour cream.
For nut lovers, sprinkle frosted cake with chopped pecans or walnuts.

Classic Cheesecake

Servings 16
Serving Size 1 slice
Calories 250
Fat 17 g
Saturated Fat 8 g
Cholesterol: 45 mg
Sodium 230 mg
Carbohydrates 21 g
Fiber 0 g
Sugar 18 g
Protein 6 g

A smooth and rich way to end any meal, this easy to whip-up decadent dessert uses Neufchâtel cheese to reduce the number of calories in each slice.

WildSide Jar

6 whole graham crackers, halved
½ C walnuts, toasted
1 ⅛ C granulated sugar, divided
2 Tbsp butter, melted
1 Tbsp water
4 lg eggs
1 tsp vanilla extract
4 (8 oz) pkgs Neufchâtel cheese

Preheat oven to 325° F. Add graham crackers and walnuts to jar and secure lid. Press "Pulse" 16-20 times until ground to fine crumbs. Remove lid and stir. Add 2 tablespoons (or ⅛ cup) sugar, butter and water and secure lid. Press "Pulse" 3-5 times. Press crust onto bottom of 9" springform pan.

Add eggs, vanilla, Neufchâtel cheese and the remaining sugar to clean jar and secure lid. Select "Batters". Pour over crust. Bake 55 minutes or until center is almost set. Cool; loosen cake from rim of pan. Refrigerate for 4 hours before serving.

Fresh Fruit Tartlets

Servings 18
Serving Size 1 tartlet
Calories 240
Fat 13 g
Saturated Fat 8 g
Cholesterol 35 mg
Sodium 35 mg
Carbohydrates 28 g
Fiber 0 g
Sugar 16 g
Protein 3 g

This is a twist on the classic French fruit tart that is both elegant and easy to prepare.
Serve with fresh seasonal fruit and top it off with the citrus glaze.

WildSide Jar

1 C unsalted butter, semi-melted
¾ C powdered sugar
¼ tsp kosher salt
2 ¼ C all-purpose flour
⅓ C heavy cream
8 oz Neufchâtel cheese, quartered
⅔ C granulated sugar, divided
½ tsp vanilla extract
¼ C fresh lime juice, approximately 2 limes

Preheat oven to 350°F. Add butter, powdered sugar, salt and flour to jar and secure lid. Press "Pulse" 8–10 times. Use spatula to scrape sides of jar to ensure all ingredients are incorporated. Press a couple tablespoons of dough into foil muffin liners. Bake in oven for 9–11 minutes until edges are lightly golden brown.

Prepare tart filling by adding cream, Neufchâtel cheese, ⅓ cup granulated sugar and vanilla to jar and secure lid. Press "Pulse" 4–6 times until ingredients are incorporated; do not over blend. Fill cooled tartlet shells with cream cheese filling. Refrigerate tartlets.

In a saucepan over the stove, stir and bring to a boil the lime juice and the remaining ⅓ cup granulated sugar. Allow the glaze to boil for 20 seconds then remove from heat and allow to cool. Garnish tartlets with desired fruit. Using a pastry brush glaze the tartlets. Serve immediately or chill until ready to serve.

For a lower fat version, substitute the Neufchâtel cheese filling with low-fat vanilla or lemon yogurt cheese. To prepare yogurt cheese, place 2 cups of yogurt in a colander lined with a couple layers of cheesecloth. Place colander over a bowl and let drain for several hours in refrigerator. The desired consistency for the flavored yogurt cheese is that of soft cream cheese.

Peach Crisp

In this recipe, you use the blender to transform whole almonds to almond meal. Almond meal provides a tasty, nutritious option for the gluten-conscious cook. Almond meal is richer in bone-building calcium, healthy unsaturated fats, vitamin E, magnesium, and dietary fiber than wheat flour.

Servings 8
Serving Size ¾ cup
Calories 270
Fat 16 g
Saturated Fat 1 g
Cholesterol 0 mg
Sodium 100 mg
Carbohydrates 28 g
Fiber 6 g
Sugar 20 g
Protein 7 g

Either Jar
½ C apple juice
½ Tbsp arrowroot powder
1 Tbsp fresh lemon juice
¼ tsp ground ginger
8 peaches, peeled, pitted and quartered
2 C almonds
1 tsp ground cinnamon, divided
½ tsp kosher salt
2 Tbsp coconut oil, melted
⅓ C turbinado sugar

Preheat oven to 350°F. In an 8" or 9" square baking dish, add first 4 ingredients and stir together. Add peaches to baking dish and toss in juice mixture. Add remaining ingredients to jar and secure lid. Press "Speed Up" to Speed 1, run cycle for 25 seconds and press "Pulse" to stop cycle. Sprinkle topping over the peaches and cover with aluminum foil. Bake for 40 minutes. Remove foil and bake an additional 5–10 minutes, until top is golden brown and juices bubble.

Try substituting ⅓ of almonds with hazelnuts.

Lemon Bars

Luscious lemon treats that are a pleasure to bring to any party or gathering.

Servings 20
Serving Size 1 bar
Calories 190
Fat 8 g
Saturated Fat 4.5 g
Cholesterol 60 mg
Sodium 100 mg
Carbohydrates 29 g
Fiber 0 g
Sugar 20 g
Protein 2 g

WildSide Jar
¾ C butter, semi-melted
⅔ C powdered sugar
1 ¾ C all-purpose flour, divided
¼ tsp kosher salt
⅓ C fresh lemon juice
4 lg eggs
½ tsp baking powder
2 C granulated sugar

Preheat oven to 350°F. Add butter, powdered sugar, 1 ½ cups flour and salt to jar and secure lid. Press "Pulse" 2–3 times until ingredients are blended. Remove lid and use spatula to scrape sides and move dough towards center of jar and secure lid. Press "Pulse" 1-2 times until all ingredients are incorporated. Press dough evenly into 9"x 13" pan. Bake for 20–25 minutes until edges of crust are lightly golden brown. Add remaining ingredients to jar and secure lid. Select "Batters". Pour lemon filling onto crust. Bake for 25 minutes or until set. Allow bars to cool and dust with powdered sugar before serving.

Frozen

Popeye's Ice Cream

Servings 8
Serving Size ½ cup
Calories 80
Fat 2.5 g
Saturated Fat 1.5 g
Cholesterol 10 mg
Sodium 20 mg
Carbohydrates 12 g
Fiber < 1 g
Sugar 9 g
Protein 1 g

A quick frozen vanilla treat with spinach that offers 20% of your daily vitamin A.

FourSide Jar
¾ C half and half
¼ C agave nectar
½ banana
⅔ C nonfat dry milk
2 C spinach, lightly packed
1 ½ Tbsp vanilla extract
2 ½ C ice cubes

Add ingredients to jar in order listed and secure lid. Select "Ice Cream" and serve.

For Pumpkin Ice Cream, follow instructions as above except substitute ½ cup pumpkin purée for the spinach, add ½ teaspoon pumpkin pie spice; increase ice to 3 cups.

For Vegan Pistachio Ice Cream, follow instructions above except substitute coconut milk for half and half and substitute 1 avocado, peeled and pitted (approximately ⅔ cup flesh) for nonfat dry milk. After the cycle is complete add ¼ teaspoon almond extract and 3 tablespoons shelled pistachios and secure lid. Press "Pulse" 3–5 times and serve.

Quick Strawberry Ice Cream

So easy to make, you can whip up a cold, creamy celebration any day of the week.

FourSide Jar
¾ C half and half
½ C sweetened condensed milk
2 Tbsp fresh lemon juice
16 oz frozen strawberries, approximately 3 C

Add ingredients to jar in order listed and secure lid. Select "Ice Cream" and serve*.

*After the "Ice Cream" cycle is complete, you may need to stir contents of jar, secure lid and press and hold "Pulse" for 3-5 seconds until smooth.

To prepare this recipe in the WildSide jar, follow the instructions below:
1 C half and half
¾ C sweetened condensed milk
2 Tbsp lemon juice
20 oz frozen strawberries, approximately 4 cups

Add ingredients to jar in order listed and secure lid. Select "Ice Cream" and serve.

Berry Sorbet

Summer time is the prime time to indulge in fresh berries. This simple sorbet is filled with very berry important nutrients.

Servings 6
Serving Size ½ cup
Calories 50
Fat 0 g
Saturated Fat 0 g
Cholesterol 0 mg
Sodium 0 mg
Carbohydrates 14 g
Fiber 2 g
Sugar 11 g
Protein < 1 g

FourSide Jar
1 C raspberries
½ C blueberries
½ C blackberries
3 Tbsp honey
2 ½ C ice cubes

Add first 4 ingredients to jar and secure lid. Select "Batters". Add ice cubes to jar and secure lid. Select "Ice Cream" and serve.

Citrus Strawberry Sorbet

A great way to enjoy a serving of fruit and get 40 mg of vitamin C. Whip up before dinner, chill in serving cups and enjoy after dinner or make and serve immediately to enjoy as a soft serve sorbet.

Servings 8
Serving Size ½ cup
Calories 70
Fat 0 g
Saturated Fat 0 g
Cholesterol 0 mg
Sodium 0 mg
Carbohydrates 18 g
Fiber 2 g
Sugar 14 g
Protein 1 g

Either Jar
2 medium oranges
¼ C honey
16 oz frozen strawberries, approximately 3 C

Add first 2 ingredients to jar and secure lid. Select "Batters". Add strawberries and secure lid. Select "Ice Cream" and serve.

Strawberry Soy Sherbet

This is a great vegan recipe for a sweet strawberry treat.

Servings 9
Serving Size ½ cup
Calories 90
Fat 0 g
Saturated Fat 0 g
Cholesterol 0 mg
Sodium 22 mg
Carbohydrates 23 g
Fiber 2 g
Sugar 19 g
Protein 1 g

WildSide Jar
1 C soy milk
1 tsp xanthan gum
½ C agave nectar
20 oz frozen strawberries, approximately 4 C

Add milk and xanthan gum to jar and secure lid. Press "Speed Up" to Speed 1 for 10–12 seconds and stop cycle by pressing "Pulse" when mixture is viscous. Add remaining ingredients in order listed and secure lid. Select "Ice Cream" and serve.

Raspberry Granita

A light and refreshing fruity, fat-free finale to any meal. Serve in chilled dishes and garnish with a few raspberries.

Servings 8
Serving Size ½ cup
Calories 130
Fat 0 g
Saturated Fat 0 g
Cholesterol 0 mg
Sodium 0 mg
Carbohydrates 34 g
Fiber 4 g
Sugar 26 g
Protein 1 g

Either Jar
2 C apple juice
¾ C prunes
2 C frozen raspberries
1 Tbsp fresh lemon juice
1 C ice cubes

Add apple juice and prunes to jar and secure lid. Select "Batters". Add remaining ingredients and secure lid. Select "Whole Juice". Pour into 9"x 13" pan and freeze for 30 minutes. Using a large spoon or fork, scrape ice crystals from edges of pan into the middle of pan. Repeat this process every 30 minutes or until mixture is frozen, forming icy flakes.

Peach Frozen Yogurt

Servings 7
Serving Size ½ cup
Calories 90
Fat 0 g
Saturated Fat 0 g
Cholesterol 0 mg
Sodium 20 mg
Carbohydrates 21 g
Fiber 1 g
Sugar 19 g
Protein 2 g

Take advantage of seasonal fresh peaches or purchase frozen fruit to make this frozen treat.

FourSide Jar

¾ C low-fat vanilla yogurt
1 medium peach, halved and pitted
¼ C honey or agave nectar
2 drops almond extract
16 oz frozen peach slices, approximately 3 C

Add first 4 ingredients to jar and secure lid. Press "Pulse" 6–8 times to blend fresh peach. Add frozen peaches and secure lid. Select "Frozen Yogurt" and serve.

For Strawberry Frozen Yogurt, use 1 cup low-fat vanilla yogurt, ⅓ cup orange juice, 3 tablespoon agave nectar and 16 oz (3 cups) frozen strawberries to jar and secure lid. Select "Frozen Yogurt" and serve.

For Pineapple Frozen Yogurt, use 1 cup low-fat vanilla yogurt, ⅓ cup orange juice, 3 tablespoon agave nectar and 16 oz (3 cups) frozen unsweetened pineapple chunks to jar and secure lid. Select "Frozen Yogurt" and serve.

For Berry Banana Frozen Yogurt, use 1 cup low-fat vanilla yogurt, 2 tablespoon lemon juice, 3 tablespoon agave nectar, 6 quarter pieces frozen bananas and 9.5 oz (2 cups) frozen berries to jar and secure lid. Select "Frozen Yogurt" and serve.

Coconut Key Lime Frozen Yogurt

With a pungent taste and strong aroma, the key lime makes this frozen delight tart and tangy with a slight undertone of coconut.

Servings 6
Serving Size ½ cup
Calories 135
Fat 5 g
Saturated Fat 2 g
Cholesterol 2 mg
Sodium 27 mg
Carbohydrates 21 g
Fiber 0 g
Sugar 19 g
Protein 3 g

FourSide Jar
¾ C low-fat vanilla yogurt
⅓ C coconut milk powder
¼ C key lime juice, approximately 7–8 key limes juiced
¼ C agave nectar
3 C ice cubes

Add first 4 ingredients to jar and secure lid. Press "Pulse" 3 times. Add ice to jar and secure lid. Select "Frozen Yogurt" and serve.

For a more rich Coconut Key Lime Frozen Yogurt, follow these instructions: Portion 3 cups low-fat vanilla yogurt in an ice cube tray and freeze until solid. Add ½ cup liquid coconut milk, ¼ cup agave nectar, ¼ cup key lime juice and frozen yogurt cubes to jar and secure lid. Select "Frozen Yogurt" and serve.

Pomegranate Frozen Yogurt

This is a sweet, yet slightly tart frozen treat with live cultures combined with the antioxidant power of pomegranates. If you have leftovers, store in the freezer to save for your next treat!

Servings 7
Serving Size ½ cup
Calories 70
Fat 0 g
Saturated Fat 0 g
Cholesterol 0 mg
Sodium 30 mg
Carbohydrates 15 g
Fiber < 1 g
Sugar 12 g
Protein 1 g

FourSide Jar
2 C pomegranate juice
2 Tbsp agave nectar
¾ tsp xanthan gum
¾ C low-fat vanilla yogurt

Add pomegranate juice, agave nectar and xanthan gum to jar and secure lid. Press "Pulse" 5–7 times until juice blend becomes more viscous. Pour the mixture into an ice cube tray and freeze until solid. Remove frozen pomegranate cubes from tray. Add vanilla yogurt and frozen juice cubes to jar and secure lid. Select "Frozen Yogurt" and serve.

For a more tart treat, omit the agave nectar.

Blueberry Ice Cream

This recipe is not for the calorie counter, but it is simply delicate and feathery with only 3 ingredients.

FourSide Jar
1 ¼ C half and half
3 Tbsp granulated sugar
12 oz frozen blueberries, approximately 2 ½ C

Add ingredients to jar in order listed and secure lid. Select "Ice Cream" and serve*.

*After the "Ice Cream" cycle is complete, you may need to stir contents of jar, secure lid and press and hold "Pulse" for 3-5 seconds until smooth.

For a Berry Cherry Ice Cream, substitute 1 cup of frozen cherries for 1 cup blueberries.

Kid Creations

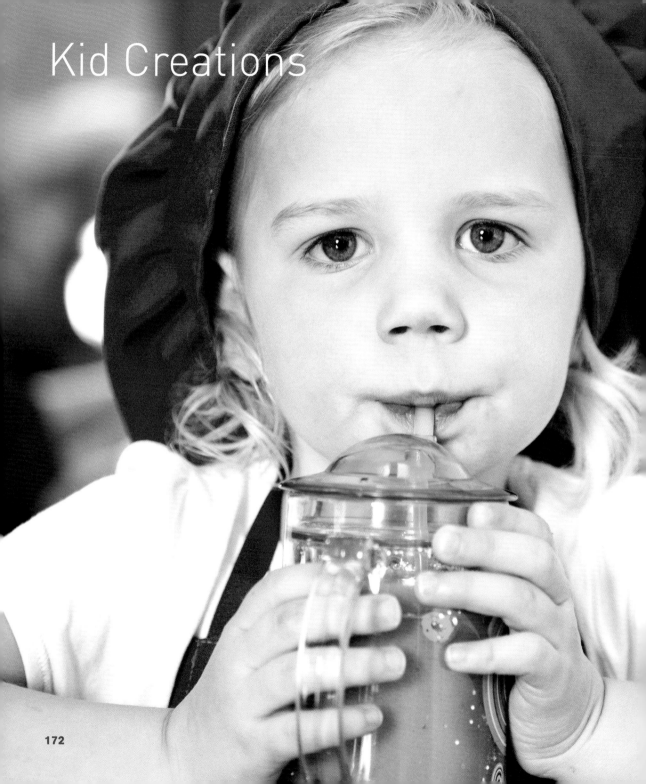

Kid Creations

Simple Banana Green Smoothie

Servings 2
Serving Size 11 fl oz
Calories 120
Fat 1 g
Saturated Fat 0 g
Cholesterol 0 mg
Sodium 45 mg
Carbohydrates 29 g
Fiber 4 g
Sugar 14 g
Protein 3 g

A great starter recipe for green smoothies. The kids love this one too; tell them it is called Green Martian Slime.

FourSide Jar

½ C water
2 bananas, halved
2 C spinach
½ C ice cubes

Add ingredients to jar in order listed and secure lid. Select "Smoothie" and serve.

Orange Grape Slushie

Servings 4
Serving Size 1 cup
Calories 140
Fat 0 g
Saturated Fat 0 g
Cholesterol 0 mg
Sodium 0 mg
Carbohydrates 34 g
Fiber 1 g
Sugar 32 g
Protein 2 g

A refreshing summer-time slushie to beat the heat and get your daily vitamin C. Have the little ones help pick and count or measure the grapes in groups of ten, approximately 60–70 grapes.

WildSide Jar

2 C red grapes
6 oz orange juice concentrate, thawed
3 C ice cubes

Add ingredients to jar in order listed and secure lid. Select "Ice Crush" and serve.

Dill Dip

Forgo the packet and preservatives, and whip this dip up in no time. Cut up any veggies you need to eat and start dill dipping. Use this dip to garnish a cream of vegetable soup or spread on bread to moisten your favorite sandwich.

FourSide Jar

1 C fat-free Greek yogurt
4 oz Neufchâtel cheese
1 tsp garlic powder
½ tsp kosher salt
1 Tbsp dried dill

Add all ingredients except dried dill to jar and secure lid. Select "Batters". Add dried dill and secure lid. Press "Pulse" 2–3 times until blended.

Try substituting the Neufchâtel cheese for 1 medium ripe avocado.

For Ranch Dip, add yogurt and Neufchâtel cheese to jar and follow instructions below:
½ tsp garlic powder
¼ tsp onion powder
¼ tsp kosher salt
⅛ tsp ground black pepper
½ tsp dried chives
½ tsp dried parsley
½ tsp dried dill

Add the garlic and onion powders, salt and pepper to jar and secure lid. Select "Dips". Add the chives, parsley and dill and secure lid. Press "Pulse" 3–5 times and serve.

Servings 12
Serving Size 2 Tbsp
Calories 35
Fat 2 g
Saturated Fat 1 g
Cholesterol 5 mg
Sodium 135 mg
Carbohydrates 1 g
Fiber 0 g
Sugar < 1 g
Protein 3 g

Berry Coconut Popsicles

Servings 8
Serving Size 1 popsicle
Calories 60
Fat 3 g
Saturated Fat 2 g
Cholesterol 0 mg
Sodium 10 mg
Carbohydrates 8 g
Fiber 2 g
Sugar 5 g
Protein 1 g

Yummy, layered frozen treats with a creamy coconut middle.

FourSide Jar
1 ⅓ C strawberries
2 Tbsp agave nectar
2 tsp fresh lemon juice, divided
¼ C low-fat vanilla yogurt
⅓ C coconut milk
2 Tbsp shredded coconut
¼ C water
1 C blueberries

Add strawberries, agave nectar and 1 teaspoon lemon juice to jar and secure lid. Press "Pulse" 4–6 times or until strawberries are blended to desired smoothness. Pour the strawberries into the popsicle mold and freeze until semi-frozen, approximately 45 minutes.

While freezing the strawberry layer, prepare the middle layer by adding yogurt, coconut milk and shredded coconut to jar and secure lid. Press "Pulse" 3–5 times. After 45 minutes, remove the popsicle mold from freezer, insert popsicle sticks and pour coconut layer over the semi-frozen strawberry layer. Return to the freezer until semi-frozen, approximately 1 hour.

Prepare the blueberry layer by adding water, blueberries, and remaining lemon juice to jar and secure lid. Select "Batters". Pour final layer of blueberry purée over semi-frozen coconut layer. Return to freezer until frozen solid, approximately 2–4 hours.

This recipe yields 8 (⅓ cup) popsicles. Have the "little ones" help count the strawberries and pluck off the strawberry stems. Depending on the size of the strawberry, there are approximately 7–8 strawberries in 1 ⅓ cup.

Orange Julicious

Servings 5
Serving Size 8 fl oz
Calories 140
Fat 1 g
Saturated Fat 0 g
Cholesterol 0 mg
Sodium 40 mg
Carbohydrates 31 g
Fiber 2 g
Sugar 28 g
Protein 4 g

A timeless, frothy and creamy classic with fresh citrus taste and the added nutrition of yellow crookneck squash.

WildSide Jar

1 C low-fat milk
2 medium oranges
1 small yellow squash, approximately 1 C
1 ½ C ice cubes
6 oz frozen orange juice concentrate
2 Tbsp honey
1 tsp vanilla extract

Add ingredients to jar in order listed and secure lid. Select "Whole Juice" and serve.

Strawberry Orange Yogurt Pops

Servings 12
Serving Size 1 popsicle
Calories 35
Fat 0 g
Saturated Fat 0 g
Cholesterol 0 mg
Sodium 10 mg
Carbohydrates 7 g
Fiber 1 g
Sugar 5 g
Protein 1 g

This natural and delightfully sweet treat is a great snack on a stick.

FourSide Jar

1 C orange juice
1 ½ C strawberries
¾ C low-fat vanilla yogurt
2 Tbsp granulated sugar

Add ingredients to jar in order listed and secure lid. Select "Batters". Pour into popsicle mold, insert popsicle sticks and freeze until solid.

Raw

Raw

Creamy Pesto Sauce

Serve this creamy pesto sauce with thin zucchini noodles. To make zucchini noodles, slice zucchini into julienne strips. To soften the zucchini noodles, salt noodles and rinse after 15 minutes. Toss noodles with this velvety pesto sauce and reserve a little avocado for garnish.

FourSide Jar

¼ C cold-pressed olive oil
3 Tbsp water
¼ tsp sea salt
1 clove garlic, quartered
1 C basil leaves, lightly packed
1 avocado, peeled and pitted
½ C pine nuts

Add ingredients to jar in order listed and secure lid. Select "Sauces" and serve immediately.

Servings 8
Serving Size 2 Tbsp
Calories 150
Fat 15 g
Saturated Fat 1.5 g
Cholesterol 0 mg
Sodium 50 mg
Carbohydrates 3 g
Fiber 2 g
Sugar 0 g
Protein 2 g

Spicy Almond Dressing

The Nama Shoyu and sesame oil give a little Asian flair to this quick and simple salad dressing. Omit half the water to make this a dip for crunchy veggies.

FourSide Jar

1 C water
3 Tbsp fresh lime juice
1 Tbsp cold-pressed sesame oil
1 Tbsp Nama Shoyu
½ C raw almonds
½ tsp cayenne pepper

Add ingredients to jar in order listed and secure lid. Select "Dressings" and serve.

Try adding 2 teaspoons of ginger root to add a little more aromatic Asian zest to this dressing.

Servings 12
Serving Size 2 Tbsp
Calories 45
Fat 3 g
Saturated Fat 0 g
Cholesterol 0 mg
Sodium 60 mg
Carbohydrates 1 g
Fiber 1 g
Sugar 1 g
Protein 1 g

Raw Red Pepper Hummus

Servings 6
Serving Size ¼ cup
Calories 160
Fat 8 g
Saturated Fat 1 g
Cholesterol 0 mg
Sodium 140 mg
Carbohydrates 18 g
Fiber 5 g
Sugar 3 g
Protein 6 g

This delectable dip has a little kick to it. Serve on squash rounds or with other crudités for a hearty snack.

FourSide Jar
2 Tbsp water
2 Tbsp cold-pressed olive oil
¼ C fresh lemon juice, approximately 2 lemons
¾ C garbanzo beans, soaked overnight and rinsed
3 Tbsp sesame seeds
½ red bell pepper, cored, seeded and quartered
2 cloves garlic, halved
1 chunk onion, approximately 2 Tbsp
1 tsp cumin
½ tsp kosher salt

Add ingredients to jar in order listed and secure lid. Press "Speed Up" to Speed 5 and run full cycle until desired consistency is reached.

Tahini Dressing

Servings 12
Serving Size 2 Tbsp
Calories 40
Fat 3.5 g
Saturated Fat 0 g
Cholesterol 0 mg
Sodium 65 mg
Carbohydrates 2 g
Fiber < 1 g
Sugar 0 g
Protein 1 g

This dressing is great for a green salad garnished with jicama and parsley.

FourSide Jar
¼ C fresh lemon juice
1 Tbsp Nama Shoyu
⅔ C water
½ C sesame seeds
2 cloves garlic
½ tsp paprika

Add ingredients to jar in order listed and secure lid. Press "Speed Up"to Speed 8, run cycle for 25 seconds and press "Pulse" to stop cycle.

Almonaise

This is a raw version of vegan mayo. Spice it up with cayenne pepper or add a little fresh basil for an herbed mayo.

Servings 24
Serving Size 1 Tbsp
Calories 60
Fat 6 g
Saturated Fat 0.5 g
Cholesterol 0 mg
Sodium 35 mg
Carbohydrates < 1 g
Fiber 0 g
Sugar < 1 g
Protein < 1 g

FourSide Jar
½ C raw almonds, soaked overnight and rinsed
½ C water
2 Tbsp fresh lemon juice
½ Tbsp raw apple cider vinegar
2 tsp raw agave nectar
⅛ tsp ground mustard
¼ tsp sea salt
½ C cold-pressed olive oil

After soaking almonds, place almond between thumb and index finger and pop off almond skin. Set aside almonds. Add ingredients to jar, except olive oil, in order listed and add skinned almonds last. Secure lid and select "Sauces". For a second cycle, remove vented gripper lid insert, select "Sauces" and add olive oil in a steady stream over duration of cycle. Use immediately or refrigerate for up to 1 week.

Raw Tuna Salad

Serve this salad on a leaf of romaine lettuce or collard leaf topped with sprouts and sliced grape tomatoes.

Servings 4
Serving Size ½ cup
Calories 230
Fat 21 g
Saturated Fat 1.5 g
Cholesterol 0 mg
Sodium 55 mg
Carbohydrates 6 g
Fiber 4 g
Sugar 2 g
Protein 7 g

Either Jar
¼ C Almonaise, see recipe above
1 Tbsp fresh lemon juice
2 stalks celery, roughly chopped
1 clove garlic, quartered
½ C sunflower seeds, soaked overnight and rinsed
⅓ C raw almonds, soaked overnight and rinsed
½ tsp dried dill
¼ tsp no-salt herb seasoning

Add ingredients to jar in order listed and secure lid. Press "Pulse" 8–10 times until desired consistency is reached; do not over blend.

Tangy Tomato Sauce

Tasty tomato sauce great on raw squash noodles or raw pizza.

FourSide Jar

¼ C cold-pressed olive oil
1 Tbsp Nama Shoyu
1 tsp raw apple cider vinegar
1 beefsteak tomato
½ C sun-dried tomatoes
¼ C onion
4 basil leaves
¼ jalapeño pepper
2 soft dates, pitted

Add ingredients to jar in order listed and secure lid. Select "Sauces" and serve.

Servings 7
Serving Size ¼ cup
Calories 100
Fat 8 g
Saturated Fat 1 g
Cholesterol 0 mg
Sodium 190 mg
Carbohydrates 7 g
Fiber 1 g
Sugar 5 g
Protein 1 g

Portabellas with Mushroom Sauce

This recipe is delicious and easy to make. Try serving these savory mushrooms and gravy with the parsnip rice for dinner.

FourSide Jar

4 lg portabella mushrooms, cleaned and stems removed
5 Tbsp Nama Shoyu, divided
½ C cold-pressed olive oil, divided
1 Tbsp dried oregano
1 stalk celery, roughly chopped, approximately ½ C
1 ¾ C mushrooms, sliced and divided; type: white, crimini, or shiitake
½ C water
1 Tbsp fresh lemon juice
½ clove garlic

Marinate the portabella caps for several hours in 4 tablespoons Nama Shoyu, ¼ cup olive oil, and oregano. Set aside half the celery and ¾ cup sliced mushrooms. Add the remaining ingredients (1 tablespoon Nama Shoyu, ¼ cup celery, 1 cup mushrooms, water, lemon juice and garlic) except portabella mushrooms to jar and secure lid. Select "Batters". Add reserved celery and mushroom to jar and stir together. Pour sauce over marinated portabella caps and serve.

Servings 4
Serving Size ½ cup
sauce and 1 cap
Calories 300
Fat 27 g
Saturated Fat 4 g
Cholesterol 0 mg
Sodium 930 mg
Carbohydrates 8 g
Fiber 4 g
Sugar 1 g
Protein 6 g

Pine Nut Pudding

Servings 4
Serving Size ½ cup
Calories 360
Fat 24 g
Saturated Fat 1.5 g
Cholesterol 0 mg
Sodium 0 mg
Carbohydrates 40 g
Fiber 4 g
Sugar 33 g
Protein 6 g

This a sweet treat for the pine nut lover. The tiny pine nut packs plenty of nutrition from Vitamin E to mono- and polyunsaturated fats. Nuts are a perfect satisfying snack that may also reduce the risk of heart disease. Try serving this soft pudding over fresh berries for breakfast or dessert.

FourSide Jar
1 C water
1 C soft dates, pitted
1 C pine nuts

Add ingredients to jar in order listed and secure lid. Select "Sauces" and serve.

Try sprinkling ground cinnamon or ground nutmeg over pudding to spice it up.

Split Second Applesauce

Servings 5
Serving Size ½ cup
Calories 70
Fat 0 g
Saturated Fat 0 g
Cholesterol 0 mg
Sodium 0 mg
Carbohydrates 19 g
Fiber 3 g
Sugar 14 g
Protein < 1 g

A quick and easy snack for the family. Gala and Fuji varieties are great selections for applesauce.

FourSide Jar
⅓ C water
1 banana
1 soft date, pitted
2 medium apples, cored and quartered
2 tsp fresh lemon juice

Add ingredients to jar in order listed and secure lid. Select "Sauces" and serve.

Raw Cranberry Sauce

Servings 7
Serving Size ½ cup
Calories 140
Fat 0 g
Saturated Fat 0 g
Cholesterol 0 mg
Sodium 0 mg
Carbohydrates 37 g
Fiber 5 g
Sugar 30 g
Protein 1 g

Cranberries show their festive hue from October to December. This tart and tangy berry is an excellent source of vitamin C and helps treat and prevent urinary tract infections. Sprinkle some chopped walnuts on this sauce for a little crunch.

FourSide Jar

½ C freshly squeezed orange juice
1 orange
1 apple, cored and quartered
1 C Medjool dates, approximately 8–10, pitted
2 C cranberries

Add ingredients to jar in order listed and secure lid. Press "Speed Up" to Speed 1 for 10 seconds and then increase to Speed 5 for 35 seconds and press "Pulse" to stop.

For a less sweet sauce, use prunes in place of dates.

Mango Lime Pudding

Servings 6
Serving Size ½ cup
Calories 110
Fat 5 g
Saturated Fat 2.5 g
Cholesterol 0 mg
Sodium 0 mg
Carbohydrates 17 g
Fiber 1 g
Sugar 14 g
Protein 2 g

A light and refreshing sweet treat. Serve it to guests over fresh fruit and garnish with shredded coconut.

FourSide Jar

2 ripe mangoes, peeled and pitted
½ C cashews, soaked for 2 hours and rinsed
1 Tbsp raw honey
1 Tbsp coconut oil
2 Tbsp fresh lime juice, approximately 1 lime juiced

Add ingredients to jar in order listed and secure lid. Select "Ice Cream". Serve immediately or portion into dessert dishes and chill until ready to serve.

Asparagus Soup

Servings 3
Serving Size 1 cup
Calories 170
Fat 10 g
Saturated Fat 2 g
Cholesterol 0 mg
Sodium 135 mg
Carbohydrates 13 g
Fiber 4 g
Sugar 4 g
Protein 7 g

The distinct flavor and aroma of asparagus are the highlight of this brightly colored and flavored soup.

Either Jar

1 lb asparagus
2 Tbsp fresh lemon juice, divided
1 ¼ C water
½ C cashews, soaked for 2 hours and rinsed
¼ tsp dried dill
¼ tsp celery seed
¼ tsp sea salt
1 clove garlic

Snap off tough ends of asparagus and discard. Cut off tender tips and marinate in 1 tablespoon of lemon juice and set aside. Cut asparagus spears in half. Add halved asparagus and remaining ingredients to jar in order listed and secure lid. Select "Soups". Serve soup and garnish with tips.

Try the soup with kelp noodles. Marinate the kelp along with the asparagus tips.

Green Spinach Soup

Servings 4
Serving Size 1 cup
Calories 100
Fat 7 g
Saturated Fat 1 g
Cholesterol 0 mg
Sodium 250 mg
Carbohydrates 9 g
Fiber 5 g
Sugar 1 g
Protein 3 g

Simple soup ready in less than 90 seconds. Garnish this soup with a little something that has crunch, such as red cabbage or red bell pepper.

WildSide Jar

2 C water
2 Tbsp fresh lime juice, approximately 1 lime juiced
1 jalapeño pepper, cored and seeded
3 ½ C spinach, lightly packed
1 large avocado, peeled and pitted
1 green bell pepper, cored, seeded and halved
1 C fresh cilantro leaves
½ tsp sea salt

Add ingredients to jar in order listed and secure lid. Select "Soups" and serve.

Red Hot Tomato Soup

Servings 5
Serving Size 1 cup
Calories 60
Fat 3 g
Saturated Fat 0 g
Cholesterol 0 mg
Sodium 170 mg
Carbohydrates 8 g
Fiber 3 g
Sugar 5 g
Protein 2 g

When summer tomatoes are so good that they need no embellishment, try them in this simple, refreshing starter. It's a great way to use up fast-ripening tomatoes.

WildSide Jar

4 beefsteak tomatoes, halved, approximately 5-6 C
1 red bell pepper, cored, seeded and quartered
1 Tbsp cold-pressed olive oil
1 ½ tsp raw apple cider vinegar
1 tsp ginger root, peeled
4 green onions, trimmed
½ tsp sea salt
¼ tsp ground cayenne pepper

Add ingredients to jar in order listed and secure lid. Select "Soups" and serve.

Corn and Cashew Chowder

This is a hearty chowder served great with flax crackers or slices of jicama for a little crunch.

Servings 5
Serving Size 1 cup
Calories 280
Fat 15 g
Saturated Fat 2 g
Cholesterol 0 mg
Sodium 407 mg
Carbohydrates 30 g
Fiber 4 g
Sugar 5 g
Protein 8 g

WildSide Jar
4 C fresh corn kernels, divided
2 C water
¾ C cashews
½ tsp raw apple cider vinegar
1 clove garlic
¾ tsp sea salt
2 Tbsp fresh cilantro leaves

Add ingredients to jar in order listed, except ½ cup corn kernels and cilantro, and secure lid. Select "Soups" and serve. Garnish soup with remaining corn kernels and cilantro.

Raw Lemon Cheesecake

Serve this luscious lemon dessert with a few fresh berries.

Servings 10
Serving Size 1 slice
Calories 430
Fat 29 g
Saturated Fat 8 g
Cholesterol 0 mg
Sodium 5 mg
Carbohydrates 36 g
Fiber 3 g
Sugar 27 g
Protein 10 g

Either Jar
1 ½ C raw almonds
¼ C shredded coconut
1 C raw agave nectar, divided
¾ C fresh lemon juice
3 C cashews, soaked overnight and rinsed
⅓ C coconut oil
1 tsp vanilla extract

Add almonds and coconut to jar and secure lid. Press "Speed Up" to Speed 2, run cycle for 35 seconds and press "Pulse" to stop cycle. Add ¼ cup agave nectar to jar and mix with spatula. Grease pie plate. Press nut mixture into pie plate and chill in refrigerator. Add remaining ingredients to jar in order listed and secure lid. Press "Speed Up" to Speed 5 and run full cycle. Using spatula, pour and spread lemon filling into crust and chill for 4 hours before serving.

Raw Cinnamon Bun Bites

Great for a weekend brunch or a nutty and moist cinnamon treat!

Servings 12
Serving Size 1 bun
Calories 220
Fat 14 g
Saturated Fat 2 g
Cholesterol 0 mg
Sodium 40 mg
Carbohydrates 18 g
Fiber 6 g
Sugar 9 g
Protein 6 g

WildSide Jar

⅔ **C raw almonds**

⅔ **C raw macadamia nuts**

1 **C flaxseeds**

1 ½ **Tbsp ground cinnamon**

¼ **tsp sea salt**

½ **C Date Paste, see page 191**

⅓ **C raisins**

¼ **C chopped walnuts**

1 **Tbsp raw agave nectar**

Cream Nut Frosting, see page 191

Add nuts, flaxseeds, cinnamon and sea salt to jar and secure lid. Press "Speed Up" to Speed 1, run cycle for 25 seconds and press "Pulse" to stop cycle. Add nut mixture to a mixing bowl with the date paste and incorporate. On parchment paper, spread nut mixture into a large rectangle with ¼" thickness. Sprinkle raisins and walnuts over flattened nut mixture and drizzle with agave nectar. Gently roll up the flattened nut mixture. Slice to 1 ¼" buns and top with Cream Nut Frosting.

Date Paste

A great whole food way to sweeten up any dish or dessert.

Servings 8
Serving Size 2 Tbsp
Calories 120
Fat 4 g
Saturated Fat 3 g
Cholesterol 0 mg
Sodium 2 mg
Carbohydrates 21 g
Fiber 2 g
Sugar 18 g
Protein 1 g

FourSide Jar
8 Medjool dates, pitted
2 Tbsp raw agave nectar
2 Tbsp coconut oil
¼ C dried apricots

Soak Medjool dates in 1 cup water for 1-2 hours. Reserve ¼ cup of soaking water and add to jar with remaining ingredients in order listed and secure lid. Select "Ice Crush". Use immediately or store in covered container in refrigerator for up to 2 weeks*.

*If storing in refrigerator, substitute coconut oil with a cold-pressed oil such as grapeseed oil.

For a more simple date paste, soak 8–10 Medjool dates in 1 cup water for 1–2 hours. Add **¼** cup soaking water and 1 cup pitted, soaked Medjool dates to jar and secure lid. Select "Ice Crush".

Cream Nut Frosting

Top off the raw cinnamon bun bites with this sweet spread. If you have any frosting leftovers, blend with fresh fruit to make a nutty fruit pudding.

Servings 6
Serving Size 2 Tbsp
Calories 120
Fat 9 g
Saturated Fat 2.5 g
Cholesterol 0 mg
Sodium 0 mg
Carbohydrates 9 g
Fiber < 1 g
Sugar 6 g
Protein 2 g

FourSide Jar
¼ C freshly squeezed orange juice
3 Tbsp raw honey
1 Tbsp coconut oil
½ C cashews, soaked overnight and rinsed
½ C raw macadamia nuts, soaked overnight and rinsed
1 Tbsp vanilla extract

Add ingredients to jar in order listed and secure lid. Select "Sauces". After cycle is complete, use a spatula to move ingredients towards center of jar and secure lid. Again select "Batters". Use or store in refrigerator for up to 3 days.

Caramel Dip

A perfect dip for autumn apples or to use as a filling for raw pecan tarts.

FourSide Jar
16 -18 Medjool dates, pitted
1 ½ Tbsp fresh lemon juice
1 ½ C water
½ C raw dark amber agave nectar or maple syrup
1 Tbsp vanilla extract
1 tsp sea salt

Soak first 3 ingredients together for 1–2 hours. Drain the dates and reserve the soaking water for a refreshing drink or to add to a green smoothie. Add soaked dates, agave nectar or maple syrup, vanilla extract and salt to jar and secure lid. Select "Dips". Serve or store in an airtight container for approximately 3 days.

Servings 16
Serving Size 2 Tbsp
Calories 110
Fat 0 g
Saturated Fat 0 g
Cholesterol 0 mg
Sodium 100 mg
Carbohydrates 29 g
Fiber 2 g
Sugar 26 g
Protein < 1 g

Tropical Ice Cream

As a nutritional superstar bursting with vitamins, minerals and enzymes, the avocado is known for its "good" fat. With the pineapple and coconut, you won't taste the avocado which lends this quick frozen treat a light green color and a smooth, buttery feel.

Either Jar
1 C coconut milk
¼ C raw agave nectar
1 small ripe avocado, approximately ½ C avocado flesh
10 oz frozen pineapple chunks, approximately 2 C
1 ½ C ice cubes

Add ingredients to jar in order listed and secure lid. Select "Ice Cream" and serve.

Servings 8
Serving Size ½ cup
Calories 150
Fat 9 g
Saturated Fat 6 g
Cholesterol 0 mg
Sodium 0 mg
Carbohydrates 16 g
Fiber 1 g
Sugar 13 g
Protein < 1 g

Almond Date Balls

Servings 16
Serving Size 1 piece
Calories 110
Fat 5 g
Saturated Fat 1 g
Cholesterol 0 mg
Sodium 16 mg
Carbohydrates 14 g
Fiber 2 g
Sugar 11 g
Protein 2 g

Although mostly seen during the holidays, almond date balls are a nutrient dense treat that can be served anytime of the year.

WildSide Jar

⅓ C dried and unsweetened shredded coconut
1 C raw almonds
⅛ tsp sea salt
½ vanilla bean, split and scrapped
8–10 Medjool dates, pitted
1 C dried pineapple pieces
¼ C dried cranberries

Add coconut to jar and secure lid. Press "Pulse" 4–6 times. Dump grated coconut onto a plate and set aside. Add almonds, salt, and vanilla bean seeds to jar and secure lid. Press "Speed Up" to Speed 1, run cycle for 20 seconds and press "Pulse" to stop cycle. Use spatula to move contents towards center of jar. Add dates and pineapple to jar and secure lid. Press "Pulse" 4–6 times until desired texture is reached. Stir in the cranberries. Roll into 1" balls and roll in coconut. Store covered in refrigerator for up to 3 days.

Piña Colada Sherbet

Servings 6
Serving Size ½ cup
Calories 70
Fat 1.5 g
Saturated Fat 1.5 g
Cholesterol 0 mg
Sodium 0 mg
Carbohydrates 15 g
Fiber 1 g
Sugar 10 g
Protein < 1 g

A simply refreshing treat with only 3 ingredients.

Either Jar

1 ⅓ C coconut water, drained from young coconut
⅓ C coconut meat, scraped from young coconut
1 ½ Tbsp raw agave nectar
16 oz frozen pineapple chunks, approximately 3 C

Add ingredients to jar in order listed and secure lid. Select "Ice Cream" and serve.

Miscellaneous

Baby

Baby Food Purées

These purées are for babies 6 months and older who are ready to start solids. Consult your pediatrician or general practitioner for specific nutritional requirements and guidelines.

FourSide Jar
First Fruit Purées:

2 cups steamed fruit:
   apples, peeled, cored and roughly chopped
   pears, peeled, cored and roughly chopped

2 cups fruit:
   avocados, peeled and pitted
   bananas, peeled
   papaya, peeled and seeded
   mango, peeled and pitted
   apricots, peeled and pitted
   peach, peeled and pitted
   nectarine, peeled and pitted

First Vegetable Purées:

2 cups steamed or baked vegetables:
  sweet potatoes, baked, peeled and roughly chopped
  butternut squash, baked, peeled and roughly chopped
  carrots or parsnips, steamed, peeled and roughly chopped
  corn or peas, steamed

Meat Purées:

2 cups boneless, cubed and cooked meat:
  chicken, beef, pork or turkey

Add liquid* and fruit, vegetable or meat of choice to jar and secure lid. Select "Batters". If mixture is too thick, remove vented gripper lid insert and add additional liquid through the vent opening. Continue blending to achieve desired consistency.

*The amount of liquid added depends on the tenderness and moisture content of the fruit and/or vegetable. The liquid can be water, formula or breast milk. To include some of the nutrients lost during steaming, use the cooking water when blending.

Many of these purées are suitable for freezing but bananas, once blended, are not suitable for freezing.

Baby Food Tips:
Steaming is one of the best ways to prepare foods to preserve vitamins and minerals. Place the food in a steam basket or colander above boiling water to cook. Save any leftover water to add to purées while blending.

Use ice cube trays to freeze pureed foods. Fill each cube with purée, just as if you were making ice cubes. Each cube should contain 1 ounce of food, approximately 2 tablespoons. When the tray is filled, cover with plastic wrap and freeze. Once frozen, pop out the cubes, store in a resealable container. It is best if food is used within 1 month.

Home prepared baby food should be tightly covered and stored in the coldest part of the refrigerator for no longer than 2–3 days.

Food should be thawed in the microwave, double boiler or refrigerator overnight.

If the food is too thick, you can add breast milk, formula or a little water. If the food is too thin, you can add instant baby cereal, mashed banana or yogurt.

Do not add sugar or salt as you cook. Pure foods will help keep your baby from developing a taste for salty and sugary foods.

Beauty

Exfoliating Mask

Exfoliating removes the surface layer of dead cells allowing your freshest skin to shine through. Depending on a few factors such as age and the climate in which you live, most women should exfoliate 1–2 times weekly and men should exfoliate 2–3 times weekly.

FourSide Jar
½ C almond or soy milk
2 Tbsp rolled oats
2 Tbsp avocado
½ C almonds

Add ingredients to jar in order listed and secure lid. Press "Speed Up" to Speed 2, blend until pasty (approximately 30 seconds) and press "Pulse" to stop cycle. This recipe yields enough for 2 masks.

Aloe Cucumber Freshener

A great way to refresh, hydrate and heal dry or slightly sun damaged skin.

FourSide Jar
¼ C aloe gel or ½ aloe leaf washed, peeled and chopped
½ cucumber, quartered

Add ingredients to jar in order listed and secure lid. Select "Batters". Apply to clean face and neck. Leave on for 10-15 minutes and rinse with cool water.

Pet

Chicken Nugget Treats

A simple bite-size chicken treat for your dog.

FourSide Jar

½ lb chicken breast halves, cubed
¾ C chicken cooking water
2¼ C wheat germ

Preheat oven to 350°F. Boil cubed chicken breast halves in water and reserve cooking water for blending. Add cooked and cubed chicken and water to jar and secure lid. Select "Batters". Add wheat germ and secure lid. Press "Pulse" until ingredients are incorporated. Roll dough into 1" balls and place on baking sheet. Use back of spoon dipped in water to slightly flatten the treat. Bake for 20–25 minutes. Yields 30 treats.

Peanut Butter Bones

If you are looking for the healthiest diet for your canine, the best way to monitor what your dog eats is homemade dog food and treats.

WildSide Jar

1 C fat-free milk
1 C peanut butter
1 Tbsp baking powder
2 C whole wheat flour

Preheat oven to 375°F. Add milk and peanut butter to jar and secure lid. Select "Batters". Add baking powder and 1 cup flour to jar and secure lid. Press "Pulse" until ingredients are incorporated. Use spatula to scrap sides and move ingredients towards center of jar. Add remaining flour and secure lid. Press "Pulse" until ingredients are incorporated. Turn out dough onto a lightly floured or oiled surface. Roll out to ¼" thickness and cut out shapes. Place on greased baking sheet and bake for 20 minutes until lightly brown. Yields 30 bones.

Uncommon Ingredients

Acaí: a fruit native to Central and South America containing high amounts of antioxidants, more specifically anthocyanins and flavonoids. Acaí is commonly labeled a "superfood" because the acaí fruit pulp's high antioxidant capacity helps to neutralize the harmful impact of free radicals. Acaí fruit pulp purée is often found in the frozen fruit section of your local health food store.

Agave Nectar: a liquid sweetener derived from the agave plant. It is sweeter than sugar and less viscous than honey. Agave nectar can be found in most well-stocked grocery stores near the honey.

Arrowroot Starch: a white starch powder. It is used as a natural thickener and is used in place of cornstarch in soups, sauces, and puddings. Arrowroot starch is often found in the bulk section of your local health food store, near the gluten-free flours and starches or found in the spice section.

Buckwheat: a fruit seed that is not a true cereal grain. Buckwheat is gluten-free and is often found in the bulk section of your local health food store.

Chinese Five Spice: a spice powder mixture native to Chinese cuisine including cinnamon, cloves, star anise, fennel and Sichuan pepper.

Coconut Milk Powder: is the result of spray drying raw coconut cream and is an alternative to fresh coconut milk. Please note that most commercial varieties of coconut milk powder contain casein, a milk protein.

Demerara Sugar: a coarse grain, unrefined sugar with a golden tint due to molasses content. Demerara sugar is often found in well-stocked grocery stores next to specialty sugars or in the bulk section.

Flaxseeds: a mighty seed found in two varieties, golden or brown. Flaxseeds are high in omega-3 fatty acids, lignans and fiber. Remember to use your Blendtec Blender to grind flaxseed before consumption because when eaten whole it is more likely to pass through digestive tract without your body being able to absorb its important nutrients. Store whole flaxseed in cool, dark place and upon grinding, store ground flaxseed in the freezer to keep it from oxidizing and losing its nutritional potency.

Dried Guajillo Chiles: a variety of chile peppers that is most commonly grown in Mexico. This variety is mild in heat and are often toasted and soaked before use in recipes. Guajillos chile peppers are found in Latin food markets or in some well-stocked grocery stores.

Guar Gum: a white, powdery substance made from the ground endosperm of guar beans. In food and beverages, it is used as a thickening, binding and stabilizing agent. Guar gum is often found next to gluten-free flours in well-stocked grocery stores.

Hemp Granola: a crunchy granola cereal containing toasted oats, rice crisps and hemp seeds. Many varieties of hemp granola are often wheat-free and can be found in the bulk section of your local health food store or well-stocked grocery store.

Hemp Seeds: a small seed that comes from the hemp plant and when hulled are soft white seeds. Hemp seeds contain a high percentage of essential fatty acids; these omega-6 and omega-3 fatty acids cannot be made by our body and must be obtained from the diet.

Liquid Pectin: a naturally occurring substance found in plant cell walls and is often extracted from citrus peel or apple pomace to thicken fruit juices and crushed fruit during making of jams and jellies. Liquid pectin is hydrated powdered pectin and may not be equally substituted for powdered pectin.

Masala: a mixture of spices either ground into a powder or paste used in South Asian cuisine.

Mascarpone Cheese: a fresh, spreadable creamy cheese originating from southern Italy. Mascarpone cheese can be found in well-stocked grocery stores near the milk section or near the gourmet/imported cheese section.

Medjool Dates: a variety of dates which are large, dark and sweet. Each date contains an elongated pit that must be removed before use in blender recipes.

Millet: a grain tiny in size and round in shape. It is most often associated with the main ingredient in bird feed. The most widely available form of millet is hulled; it is often found in the bulk section of well-stocked grocery stores or health food stores.

Nama Shoyu: an unpasteurized soy sauce often used in raw food cuisine. Nama shoyu is most often found in well-stocked grocery stores or health food stores in the Asian section.

Neufchâtel Cheese: a soft, unripened cheese originating from France. The American version of Neufchâtel cheese is similar to regular cream cheese yet 33% lower in fat and is higher in moisture content. Neufchâtel cheese is found near the cream cheese at your local grocery store.

Nutritional Yeast: an inactive yeast that is yellow in color and has a nutty cheesy taste. This ingredient is popular among vegans due to the unique cheesy flavor it lends to recipes. Nutritional yeast is most often found in the bulk section of your local health food store.

Quinoa: a small seed originating from a grain-like crop in the Andean region of South America often used in gluten-free cooking and baking. This tiny seed is also unique because it is a complete protein, providing the essential amino acids our bodies cannot synthesize. Quinoa is most often found near the gluten-free flours in well-stocked grocery stores or in the bulk section of your local health food store.

Red Curry Paste: a common curry paste made up of dry chili pepper, shallot, garlic, galangal or ginger, lemon grass, cilantro root, peppercorn, coriander, salt, shrimp paste and Kaffir lime zest. Red curry paste is most often found in the Asian section of well-stocked grocery stores.

Sorghum: a common cereal crop that is often ground into sorghum flour and is commonly used in gluten-free cooking and baking. Most often found near gluten-free flours in well-stocked grocery stores.

Soy Flour: a fine flour ground from soy beans. Soy flour is often used as a dough conditioner due to its high protein content (35% protein) when comparing to all-purpose flour (10-12% protein). Soy flour is often found in well-stocked grocery stores next to specialty gluten-free flours or in the bulk section or your local health food store.

Spelt: a non-hybrid grain related to wheat. Use spelt in anything in which wheat flour is used. Spelt does contain gluten yet it is appropriate and tolerated by those with wheat allergies. Spelt grains are most often found in the bulk section of your local health food store or find spelt flour near specialty flours in the baking aisle of well-stocked grocery stores.

Spirulina: a type of blue-green algae that is considered a dietary supplement and is most commonly sold in powdered form. Spirulina is most often found in the supplement section of your local health food store.

Sucanat: a brand name for a variety of whole sugar cane juice that has been heated and dried to porous granules. This natural sugar is brown in color and has a rich molasses flavor. Sucanat is often found in well-stocked grocery stores next to specialty sugars or in the bulk section of your local health food store.

Tahini: a Middle Eastern paste made from ground sesame seeds. The paste can be made in your Blendtec Blender, see page 97, or it is most often found in the Asian aisle or near the peanut butter in a well-stocked grocery stores or health food stores.

Tamari: a type of soy sauce with a fuller, richer flavor. Tamari is wheat-free and is often found next to the soy sauce at your local grocers.

Tamarind Paste: a paste made from the pulp that surrounds the mature tamarind pod. Tamarind paste is often found in Asian or Middle Eastern markets.

Teff: a very small grain originating from Ethopia. This tiny grain is gluten-free and is most often found either whole or ground; look for the whole grain in the bulk section of your local health food store or teff flour near the specialty gluten-free flours.

Tomatillo: an acidic green tomato-like fruit often used in Mexican cuisine. Tomatillos are surrounded by an inedible, paper-like husk. When selecting tomatillos, choose firm, bright-green colored tomatillos. Tomatillos are the main ingredient found in salsa verde. They are most often found in Latin food markets or in the produce section of well-stocked grocery stores.

Turbinado Sugar: a less processed sugar with larger crystals than granulated white sugar. It is often referred to as "raw sugar". It is light brown in color and retains some molasses flavor. Turbinado sugar is often found in well-stocked grocery stores next to specialty sugars or in the bulk section.

Whole White Wheat Flour: a variety of whole wheat flour ground from hard white wheat. Generally there are three classifications of wheat: red vs. white, winter vs. spring and hard vs. soft. The most commonly stocked 100% whole wheat flour on grocery store shelves is hard, red winter wheat. Red wheat has a stronger, more robust flavor than white wheat. Winter wheat and spring wheat have different growing seasons. Hard wheat contains more protein thus producing more gluten than soft wheat. Soft wheat has a higher starch content and is used to make pastry flour. Various recipes throughout the book call for whole white wheat flour, referring to hard, white wheat. It is becoming more common for well-stocked grocers to carry 100% whole white wheat flour. Some recipes call for whole white wheat flour or whole wheat flour. These flours are interchangeable; just keep in mind whole white wheat has a slightly milder flavor.

Xanthan Gum: a food thickening agent and/or stabilizer to keep foods from separating. Xanthan gum is often used in gluten-free baking to mimic the role of gluten providing structure and helping to retain gas as gluten-free breads bake. Xanthan gum is most often found near gluten-free flours in a well-stocked grocery store or health food store.

Yogurt Cheese: a soft cheese made from yogurt with most of the whey drained from it. It is a healthy alternative to cream cheese and sour cream. Yogurt cheese can be made from putting original yogurt in several layers of cheesecloth or in a paper coffee filter then set in a mesh strainer over a bowl and allowed to drain.

Young Coconut: a green coconut also known as a Thai coconut. Most young coconuts found in the store have the outer green husk removed, exposing a white layer of fibrous material and the young coconut is then wrapped in plastic wrap. Young coconuts are often used for their coconut water and tender white meat. Young coconuts are often found in Thai markets or in the refrigerated produce section of your local health food store.

Recipe Index

Ingredient Index

R

Raspberries 7, 35, 59, 77, 115, 165, 166
Red Bell Pepper 18, 93, 182, 188
Rye Flour 136, 137

S

Sesame Seeds 53, 97, 119, 182
Spinach 12, 13, 14, 15, 68, 121, 163, 173, 188
Strawberries XIII, XVI, 4, 5, 7, 9, 17, 27, 34, 35, 59, 60, 77, 81, 115, 164, 165, 166, 167, 175, 177
Sweet Potatoes 106, 120, 197

T

Tofu 83, 120
Tomato 18, 87, 106, 109, 110, 184, 188

W

Walnuts 44, 51, 107, 129, 131, 153, 156, 190
White Beans 68, 114
Whole Wheat Flour XIV, XX, 40, 48, 42, 43, 44, 47, 49, 127, 129, 130, 131, 133, 134, 135, 136, 137, 138, 155, 201

Y

Yogurt XIV, XX, XXI, 6, 8, 10, 33, 47, 69, 72, 98, 115, 159, 167, 168, 174, 175, 177

Z

Zucchini 108, 131

 Classification Icon Key XXX-XXI